New Pathfinder 3

WITHDRAWN

Impact on learning

Other titles in the series

Raising the standard
Addressing the needs of gifted and talented pupils (NPF1)
Anneli McLachlan

The language of success
Improving grades at GCSE (NPF2)
Dave Carter

CILT, the National Centre for Languages, seeks to support and develop multilingualism and intercultural competence among all sectors of the population in the UK.

CILT serves education, business and the wider community with:
- specialised and impartial information services;
- high quality advice and professional development;
- expert support for innovation and development;
- quality improvement in language skills and service provision.

CILT is a charitable trust, supported by the DfES and other Government departments throughout the UK.

NEW PATHFINDER

3

Impact on learning

What ICT can bring to MFL in KS3

CLAIRE DUGARD &
SUE HEWER

The views expressed in this publication are the authors' and do not necessarily represent those of CILT.

First published 2003 by CILT, the National Centre for Languages, 20 Bedfordbury, London WC2N 4LB

Copyright © CILT 2003

ISBN 1 904243 15 0

Printed in Great Britain by Hobbs

CILT Publications are available from: **Central Books,** 99 Wallis Rd, London E9 5LN. Tel: 0845 458 9910. Fax: 0845 458 9912. On-line orders: www.centralbooks.co.uk. Book trade representation (UK and Ireland): **Broadcast Book Services,** Charter House, 29a London Rd, Croydon CR0 2RE. Tel: 020 8681 8949. Fax: 020 8688 0615.

contents

Introduction

The focus of this book is on effective practice in Key Stage 3 (KS3) through the appropriate use of Information and Communications Technology (ICT), both in whole-class settings and by pupils working alone or in small groups. Over the last decade, a series of national initiatives have focused on raising standards of teaching and learning, the latest of which is the Key Stage 3 Strategy. The Strategy is currently being introduced in schools in England (August 2003), hence our focus at this time on how ICT can help teachers to respond to some of the particular challenges facing them in this Key Stage. Our thinking is driven by pedagogy rather than technology and frequent reference is therefore made to the KS3 Strategy and preceding initiatives, as described below. Detailed documentation on such initiatives is available on the Internet and these and all other references throughout this book can be found in the list of websites on p84. This list can also be accessed at **www.cilt.org.uk/publications/impactonlearning**, where you can follow live links through to the relevant Web pages. These links will be updated from time to time as resources change location and technology and pedagogy continue to develop.

The developing curriculum

If we take a moment to trace developments over the last few years in terms of their impact on Modern Foreign Languages (MFL) in KS3, it is clear that the advent of the National Curriculum and SATs have opened up new opportunities. Teachers in secondary schools now have ready access to detailed information regarding the achievement of new Year 7 pupils, which enables them to make differentiated demands on pupils early in their MFL course. Teachers now also know the kinds of things that pupils have done in their primary school curriculum, which in turn enables them to exploit existing relevant knowledge, skills and understanding. In the chapters that follow, we shall discuss how to use ICT to provide differentiated activities based on both ability and aptitude as well as how to exploit pupils' existing ICT skills to improve the quality of their learning in Key Stage 3.

Building on the introduction of the National Curriculum and SATs, the Government developed the National Numeracy and Literacy Strategies to raise standards in these areas. Both emphasised the importance of whole-class teaching and techniques were developed to support this mode of teaching, which are now to be applied to Key Stage 3 lessons. The implementation of the National Literacy Strategy also coincided with some strategic re-thinking about the place of grammar in MFL teaching and learning, which resulted in the requirement in the revised National Curriculum for MFL that pupils should acquire knowledge and understanding of grammar of the target language (TL). Year 7 pupils are increasingly bringing with them knowledge about language and usage. It is clear that such knowledge will help them in their MFL work, especially if it is consciously and systematically exploited. *Impact on learning* examines how this linguistic knowledge can be extended across KS3, both in a whole-class and an independent learning context.

The two National Strategies for Numeracy and Literacy have also fostered in children a reflective approach to their work and provided them with techniques to monitor their own performance, to identify problems and to take appropriate remedial action. ICT can be exploited to develop these and other study skills in KS3 as we will discuss in detail in Chapter 2.

The new focus on KS3

The reality is that the scope and pace of change at Key Stage 3 is increasing considerably. Many teachers are already involved in implementing the Strategy, which includes generic issues to be addressed at whole-school and departmental level and specific training for teachers in the Foundation Subjects Strand, where

Modern Foreign Languages is housed. The Strand's principles for teaching and learning are consistent with those informing the rest of the Strategy and are summarised in the table below taken from the Standards website:

The Principle	The Action
Focus the teaching	Plan to objectives
Provide challenge	Set expectations and teach to them so that pupils surpass previous levels of achievement
Make explicit concepts and conventions	Use questioning, explaining, modelling
Structure the learning	Use starters, plenaries and a clear lesson structure
Make learning active	Provide tasks in which pupils make meaning, construct knowledge and develop understanding and skills through problem-solving, investigation and enquiry
Make learning engaging and motivating	Use stimulating activities and materials
Develop well-paced lessons with high levels of interaction	Use collaborative tasks and talk for learning
Support pupils' application and independent learning	Use prompts, frames and scaffolds
Build reflection	Teach pupils to think about what and how they learn

ICT has a contribution to make to effective practice in MFL in all of the above areas, as we will demonstrate in the chapters which follow. These Foundation Strand headings are used as a basis for a look at whole-class teaching in Chapter 4.

Uniquely to the Foundation Subjects Strand, a non-statutory Framework has been developed to assist teachers in their delivery of MFL at KS3. The structure of the Framework for MFL itself reflects that of the National Literacy Strategy, in that it also involves work at word, sentence and text level. The Framework consists of year-on-year objectives grouped under five headings, with guidance on using the objectives and on effective teaching approaches. The five headings are as follows:

- words;
- sentences;
- texts: reading and writing;
- speaking and listening;
- cultural knowledge and content.

The focus is on thoughtful lesson planning around a cluster of objectives drawn from these headings – it is not a syllabus which teachers should work through systematically. The Framework is underpinned by a set of general principles about language and language learning, in addition to the Foundation Strand principles tabled above, all of which we will apply to ICT-based activities as appropriate throughout the book.

So, there is a great deal of external input to occupy the MFL teachers' minds, to say nothing of their own aspirations for their pupils in Key Stage 3. We hope that what follows will ease the burden! We shall begin by discussing the generic features of ICT likely to add value to MFL teaching and learning, before moving on to actual applications aimed at developing pupil study skills, promoting effective language acquisition and enhancing whole-class teaching.

Making the most of ICT in the MFL classroom

- ☐ Why should I use ICT in my teaching?

- ☐ Should I expect any changes in classroom dynamics?

- ☐ Can ICT expand opportunities for pupil key skills development?

- ☐ How can ICT make me more efficient when it takes longer to plan ICT lessons?

- ☐ How can I manage the use of ICT by KS3 pupils?

chapter 1

Why should I use ICT in my teaching?

ICT in education

Since the introduction of the National Grid for Learning (NGfL) in 1998 (now the ICT in Schools initiative), a staggered programme of Government funding to promote the use of Information and Communications Technology (ICT) in education, it has been clear that ICT is at the heart of the current Government's vision for raising standards. We have seen huge investments in hardware, which have equipped primary and secondary schools with computers and connection to the Internet, with Broadband on its way for all schools. Considerable investment from the New Opportunities Fund (NOF) lottery money has gone into subject-specific ICT training for teachers. Websites such as TeacherNet and the Virtual Teacher Centre, have been established to develop networks of educational professionals and Curriculum Online, with its aim of providing high-quality electronic teaching resources for all curriculum subjects across the key stages, is one of the latest initiatives to empower teachers in their use of ICT in subject teaching.

At the same time, ICT as a subject and a teaching medium across the curriculum has become a daily reality for pupils and as such features in the compulsory core of the KS3 National Strategy. The National Curriculum specifies the statutory requirement for pupils to apply and develop their use of ICT to support their learning in all subjects, including Modern Foreign Languages (MFL). The belief that ICT can contribute to more effective learning and increased opportunities is also reflected by its high profile in the Languages Strategy for England, published by the DfES at the end of 2002.

The vision for all this modernisation is aimed not only at raising standards of teaching and learning and preparing teachers and pupils for the reality of the 21st century, but also at reducing teacher workloads and maximising resources. As a result of the many initiatives focused on ICT, the UK has become a world leader in the use of ICT in education and research projects over a number of decades have highlighted a number of areas in which ICT can positively influence language learning. So what is the impact of this investment of Government resources and teacher time likely to be in the MFL classroom?

ICT and its impact on MFL

Differing learning styles

When a teacher is asked why computers are valuable as part of the teaching and learning process, it is not uncommon to hear one of the following in reply:

- 'My pupils love using computers, particularly the boys.'
- 'They get excited when I take them to the computer suite.'
- 'They like doing work on screen, they much prefer computers to writing on paper.'

It is certainly true that a motivated pupil is better disposed to learn more effectively using ICT, but we are missing crucial opportunities to develop our pupils' skills and knowledge if we do not recognise where and **how** ICT can add to the language-learning experience beyond simple motivation.

The cognitive processes of working on screen are different from working on paper. When drafting directly into a Word document, for example, pupils can take more risks with new language, as errors can easily be corrected in response to teacher feedback or re-evaluation as they work. Feedback is immediate rather than two weeks hence. The skills of learning to learn are examined in detail in Chapter 2, but it is worth taking a moment to refer to the five distinct learning styles identified by Gardner (1983) – visual, auditory, kinaesthetic, analytic and holistic.

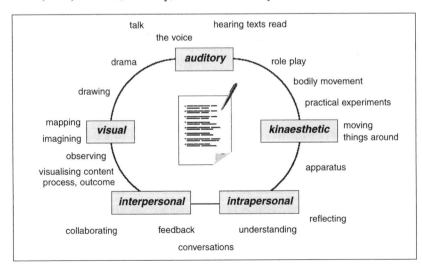

Source: Gardner (1983)

It is commonly accepted that while we each may have one or more preferred learning styles, all of us benefit from a teaching approach which incorporates a range of activity types. For example, you may not consider yourself to have a strength in kinaesthetic learning, but try a little experiment suggested in the DfES booklet *Learning styles and writing in MFL* (DfES 2002).

> *To experience the link between hand movement and thought, try explaining something without gesture ...*

Most of us will find such a task difficult or uncomfortable to achieve. The facility to delete words and move them around the screen can both appeal to a kinaesthetic learning style and represent the logical thought processes a learner must go through to achieve accurate grammar. The following example (based on Rendall 2003) could be attempted in English or the target language (TL), depending on your learners:

1 Translate the sentence *Je mange les frites* ➡ I eat chips.
2 Change 'I eat chips' to include a pronoun ➡ I eat **them.**
3 Which word have you disposed of? ➡ *chips.*
4 Remove *frites* in French and what are you left with? ➡ *Je mange **les.***
5 *Les* is your pronoun, but in French this has to move to go before the verb.
6 Drag and drop the pronoun into the correct place ➡ *Je **les** mange.*

This explanation has the added advantage of offering an alternative to formal and daunting rules, while retaining use of the correct grammatical terminology.

Hitting all the buttons!

In appealing to visual learning tendencies, colour can be used to highlight grammatical concepts, such as gender. As well as in language introduction, this can be particularly useful during the 'practice' phase, where pupils are given the opportunity to 'play' with language before being asked to manipulate it – many young learners find it very demanding to jump straight from the passive introduction stage to active manipulation. For example, pupils who have been taught French masculine nouns with the text coloured in blue will find it easier to start completing sentences using the correct partitive article, where *du* is also coloured in blue on screen.

The visual support of graphics, both static and animated, to reinforce the target language can lead to improved language retention and increased confidence in pupils. Sound files can be used in a similar way, such as a miaow to accompany *le chat,* or access to the spoken form of written language whenever required. Even the screen position of language or the direction it enters the screen from can be exploited to reinforce teaching points.

A significant and very positive feature of multimedia is, therefore, its facility to appeal to a variety of learning styles simultaneously. As the capacity of technology increases, we are also seeing more opportunities for the incorporation of video, which brings the added benefit of exposure to images, attitudes and behaviour particular to the culture of the TL country or countries. Where multimedia is further combined with interactivity, such as on a CD-ROM (see example below), Web-based activities or exercises created in authoring software, whole new dimensions in language learning are opened up. Immediately pupils have access to regular feedback and opportunities for repetition and learner independence. A computer never tires of going over the same ground and can give its user unlimited attention and feedback, an impossible feat for a classroom teacher. Pupils are also more willing to go over the same point again and again, in a way they would not do when working in a more traditional environment.

Source: *Métro Electro* (Heinemann, 2003)

This immediate feedback allows pupils to progress at a much faster pace and can appeal to pupils' competitive spirit, as score totals are usually displayed on screen, sometimes accompanied by celebratory sound effects or print-out certificates. Chapter 2 explores independence in language learning in more detail, by making pupils explicitly aware of how to learn.

An increasing range of resources are available to the MFL teacher, both in terms of the technology for lesson delivery and also software. For example, well-known and readily available generic applications such as word-processing, data-processing, e-mail, Web browser and presentation software, as well as subject-specific software. A suggestion is also made in Chapter 2 for the use of moderated on-line discussions using bulletin or notice boards, although this may be a very new area for some teachers and pupils. This book does not attempt to cover all resources but instead considers a number of language-learning contexts particularly relevant in KS3 where ICT has the potential for significant impact. As with all the tools in a languages toolkit, integration of ICT into a lesson or series of lessons is the key for effective teaching and learning. Language-learning objectives need to be clear and shared with pupils and ICT tasks should provide cognitive as well as linguistic challenges, whether ICT be used specifically for language practice, for communication or for the preparation of presentation-quality material. The development of ICT in the National Curriculum has meant that for several years now pupils have been entering Year 7 with an increased awareness of ICT concepts and practical skills. There will be differentiated needs in ICT, as well as in MFL, which are touched upon towards the end of this chapter, but first and foremost an MFL teacher needs to ensure that the maximum amount of valuable lesson time is devoted to language learning.

Should I expect changes in classroom dynamics?

New classroom relationships

The use of ICT can have significant impact on classroom relationships. This influence is often very positive and sometimes even surprising, thanks to the change of focus, support for learning, diverse resources and extra facilities it offers. To a certain degree, the ICT facilities available will influence the extent and nature of this impact, but whatever the level of resourcing, teachers should ideally plan lessons to include a variety of contexts within which to work, such as the whole class, pairs and groups of similar ability and mixed ability. Where you are creating opportunities via ICT for pupils to learn in a context of social interaction, you are also enabling them to share their styles of learning and strategies for understanding and retaining language, which can take them further more quickly. In the context of the KS3 National Strategy, we find the message: 'in their efforts to negotiate meaning, learners gain a firmer grasp of concepts and increase their range of ways to express them' (DfES 2002). It is certainly true to say that we often need to talk something through to know what we think and to understand new concepts.

The context of whole-class teaching is considered in more detail in Chapter 4, but where more independent access is available, pupils can be set to work in pairs on drafting or editing a text, for example, where collaboration is encouraged by the fact that ideas can be tested and adopted/easily rejected and mistakes can be quickly rectified. This flexibility of working can facilitate new pairings within a class where pupils who would not usually choose to sit next to one another can discover successful ways of working together. Where pupils are creating a PowerPoint presentation, for example, one pupil may bring better technical skills and the other more sophisticated linguistic understanding. Where a pair is completing a simulation task on the Internet, one pupil may have a greater grasp of the culture or history of the target language country and lead his or her more linguistically-talented partner through the target language text, by applying logic based on this knowledge. This type of thinking and working tends not to happen so easily when pupils are confined to the limited and predictable content and static presentation of the class coursebook. This is all good news for teachers who only have access to fewer computers than pupils!

More dynamic groupings

Groupwork can bring into play an interesting division of labour and responsibilities to the rest of the group. This can provide motivation where there may be limited intrinsic interest in the actual task. An e-mail project is a good example, where a topic is split into a sub-topic per group:

```
Ma ville
Groupe 1:    Divertissements
Groupe 2:    Sports et loisirs
Groupe 3:    Histoire
Groupe 4:    Magasins
Groupe 5:    Enseignement
```

One pair within a group may devise questions to pose to their TL partner school group, while another pair builds up a list of new vocabulary based on incoming messages, and another researches the local information requested by the partner school.

All these activities are interdependent, as outcomes must be shared within the group to enable work to progress. Ultimately, outcomes need to be developed to presentation quality to be shared with the whole class. This exchange of new information on a topic will be crucial to the progress of the class as a whole and its existence in electronic form means that it can easily be shared. Once shared, the information can be improved, merged, personalised, edited to reflect individual needs or rejected and deleted by each pupil. The above project also provides an opportunity for TL communication for a real purpose, which can sometimes be difficult to achieve in the MFL classroom.

Chapter 4 explores the particular features of successful whole-class teaching which have been facilitated by recent developments in presentation technologies. The advent of handy peripherals, such as the optical wireless mouse, the graphics tablet and the wireless keyboard, which allow the teacher to control what is happening on screen from anywhere in the classroom, means that the focus can switch fully from the teacher to the language on screen. A computer can take on a more neutral role than the teacher and can encourage participation from unlikely candidates. Pupils can take risks and expose their thought processes to other pupils and misconceptions or areas of difficulty can be spotted immediately and discussed in a cognitive fashion, with the teacher facilitating.

Coping with KS3 mixed ability

Working with ICT can support pupils with a variety of special needs. Specialist software and hardware is available for those with severe needs – the BECTA website offers extensive material and links relating to this area. Some software has also been adapted specifically to support MFL, such as *Writing with Symbols* from Widgit and *Clicker* from Crick Software.

Source: Writing with Symbols 2000 (Widgit)

General features of the ICT found in nearly all schools, however, can support pupils who demonstrate less severe needs. For example, teachers have the option of increasing the size of the font of text on screen for pupils with certain types of visual impairment, whether in front of the whole class or for independent work. A pastel-coloured background can replace the stark quality of pure white and more legible font colours can be used. Beware of certain colour combinations, however – useful advice on writing for the screen is available on the ICT4LT site.

Pupils who have difficulty with handwriting can be supported by regular work on screen in Word, for example. Such pupils rarely get beyond the first couple of questions on a paper-based worksheet and are unlikely to take pride in what they achieve via this process. When completing a worksheet on screen, however, they merely need to type letters or copy and paste a correct answer from a pool of answers. Handwriting can thus be removed as a barrier to linguistic progression, as lesson time is spent thinking about language rather than physically copying out. The language that such a pupil is able to produce, in whatever format, will ultimately be of a higher and more rewarding quality.

There are also significant advantages for the teacher when preparing materials. An electronic document can be saved in different versions, each aimed at a different sub-group of a class. A good worksheet is characterised by clear progression in linguistic challenge as pupils work through the activities and, in electronic form, questions can be easily removed and/or added at either end to differentiate by volume and difficulty of content. You can also differentiate by support – for example, you might remove the pool of words which accompany a gap-fill activity for your most able. You can also provide optional comments, where pupils can rest their mouse on a highlighted word to see the English translation appear, if needed, in a reading exercise (in Word, go to Insert > Comment).

Can ICT expand opportunities for pupil key skills development?

While language teaching and learning should always be the focus of MFL lessons, the use of ICT can and should simultaneously develop proficiencies, knowledge and awareness of significant value to pupils in the context of key life skills. As pupils become aware of the range of skills and experiences in play, their level of motivation for MFL lessons can only increase, which will have a positive impact on achievement.

When using the Internet, for example, they realise how quick, cheap and easy it can be to communicate with people at great distance. It may provide their first opportunities for communicating with people from other countries, developing positive attitudes and empathy as they realise they are real people with real concerns similar to their own. If pupils in different countries collaborate on a website project, for example, they will be discussing issues, sharing opinions and negotiating, developing their skills for working with others in a much broader context than might usually be the case. A wider range of ICT, such as video-conferencing, document sharing over the Web and synchronous chat, may also come into play – see InfoTech 7: *Communicating on-line* (Gläsmann 2004) as a source of more detailed information on the use of communication technologies for MFL. Where communication is via audio, they may realise that their pronunciation is unclear to non-native English speakers and devise strategies to combat this. Exposure to such elements can provide insights into the scope and direction a pupil's own life might take and the global options available to him or her. In addition, pupils gain insight into the power of international communication and their potential for conducting business in an international context.

Pupils can be exposed subliminally to many aspects of TL culture(s), through headlines, photographs, video clips and humorous cartoons, for example, particularly via the Internet. Such data is likely to be up-to-date and contributes greatly to pupils' international awareness. The enormous scope of material on the Web means that content relevant to pupils' age and interests can be identified and valuable skills of discernment and decision-making can be developed as pupils opt for which material to work with. Language work can be personalised, such as in the use of a TL horoscope for a particular day or through an Internet search for material on a pupil's hobby, which both motivates and contributes to language-learning skills.

The use of alternative contexts for language work varies the pupil diet and underpins the message that information can be expressed in different ways for different audiences, for example in a spreadsheet, database, PowerPoint presentation or e-mail message, where the register of language in each is likely to be very different. A topic-based approach to MFL teaching could be enhanced by working with similar information and target language through a variety of media across a series of lessons. Some of these concepts clearly evoke the National Curriculum Programme of Study for MFL, but there is interesting overlap with that for ICT also. As well as developing core ICT skills, pupils are forming conclusions about what, how and to whom they present information. There is also significant potential for promoting pupil presentation skills, which is developed in Chapter 4.

Processing information existing in different forms develops both linguistic and cognitive skills. Skimming and scanning, reading for gist and/or detail, coping with unknown language, summarising and expanding are all valuable information-handling skills. As pupils seek to communicate in new contexts, they are exercising problem-solving skills, developing their ability to apply and adapt their knowledge of the TL. The flexibility of electronic text enables pupils to redraft their work, to reflect on and improve their own learning and performance. The existence of commercial software to support linguistic development, as detailed in Chapter 3, also has a significant contribution to make.

How can ICT make me more efficient when it takes longer to plan ICT lessons?

It is fair to say that ICT skills and confidence take time to develop and that initial attempts could well be negatively disproportionate to the added value to the learning achieved as a result. While searching on the Internet is amazingly quick, the process of sifting and evaluating material can be very time-consuming. When the wider and longer term view is taken, however, it is easy to see how the use of ICT can save teachers time in the long run and raise standards in teaching and learning.

Sharing higher-quality resources

The flexibility of electronic resources offers many advantages:

- teachers can differentiate materials easily for specific pupils and/or classes;
- a resource can be edited after a lesson for improvements and corrections – it is then more likely to be used year on year and will be better quality as a result;
- teachers can include graphics to improve clarity and presentation of a resource, again extending access to a wider range of learning styles;
- high-quality, professional-looking materials are more likely to be shared with colleagues within the department or further afield, such as on an LEA Intranet, a national on-line teachers' network such as Lingu@NET Forum or the Teacher Resource Exchange;
- colleagues can edit shared resources to suit their own teaching styles or specific objectives;
- teaching resources can be saved onto the school network for pupils to access for revision;
- those topics affected most by the passage of time can be kept up-to-date, through exploitation of Internet-based sources;
- authentic and culturally-specific information and resources can be integrated more consistently into teaching materials. For example, a 30-second video clip can be

accessed very quickly through a hyperlink in a Word document or specialised information of interest to the pupils can be quickly sourced on the Internet and integrated into a PowerPoint presentation (e.g. on a martial art, the current vogue in music or football stars).

The Internet in particular, with its huge range of authentic resources in a variety of media formats, can be significantly exploited. Internet-based text can be copied and pasted into a Word document and then edited to an appropriate level of language. It is, of course, good practice to include the source URL on a worksheet, which also reinforces to the pupil that the text they are reading is current and authentic. It is important at all times to be clear about the issues of copyright and intellectual property rights when using materials sourced from the Web. Refer to the DfES Superhighway Safety website for more information.

A few tips for maximising efficiency

Constant re-invention of the wheel can be avoided by sharing resources and teachers are thus exposed to opportunities to consider their own and others' teaching styles. Collaboration across a department is to be particularly encouraged and can have significant time-saving benefits, although it does involve some planning and organisation. Before embarking on departmental development of ICT resources, multilateral agreements on who will do what and how resources will be exploited need to be made:

- Build up a bank of images and sound files centrally to facilitate consistency (where non-culturally specific) and to avoid overlap, time-consuming searching and potential pupil confusion.
- Agree on the use of colour within and across languages (e.g. to represent gender).
- Share useful templates (e.g. a PowerPoint presentation on weather, which can easily be adapted for all languages).
- Research existing ready-made resources, in particular textbook publishers' websites, other school websites with MFL pages and the Teacher Resource Exchange.
- Establish a coherent system of file naming from the start, so that valuable files are not over-written and teachers do not have to open a document to find out what is contained within.

Where funds are limited for the purchase of commercial materials, pupils can still be provided with professional-looking resources through the use of ICT, which can have important implications for the status of MFL as a subject within a school.

How can I manage the use of ICT by KS3 pupils?

Your school ICT Co-ordinator should be able to tell you what National Curriculum level your pupils are working at in ICT, as well as the specific applications with which they are familiar. Some pupils will still need support, however, so do have ICT instructions available – adapt instructions already used for teaching ICT, preferably so that it is in the TL and illustrated. You can create a 'screen dump' by clicking Shift – Print Screen or Alt – Shift – Print Screen and then pasting the image into your instructions sheet. As in any MFL lesson, a clear list of activities to be completed with examples for pupils to refer to will be invaluable. Try not to abandon use of the TL when in the computer suite – the visual support available should promote **more** TL use! BECTA provides 'Say IT' sheets in a number of MFL and Community Languages with TL phrases for the MFL computer suite, which can be blown up in size and used as posters.

The benefits in terms of social dynamics of grouping together pupils with complementary skills were mentioned earlier, but this can also alleviate the problem of individual pupils needing ICT support. Another approach is to identify a number of more ICT-skilled pupils who can take turns to be designated 'helpers' over a series of lessons – this cooperation can then be acknowledged via your school's reward system. Different-coloured markers are made available in the ICT suite, which can be placed on top of a pupil's computer when he or she needs assistance. A red marker can mean he or she needs linguistic help from the teacher, a blue marker can mean he or she needs peer ICT support, for example. If you are lucky enough to have a languages technician at your disposal, he or she could fit neatly into this type of approach – if you don't, investigate the potential of support from your sixth-form students, Learning Support or Foreign Language Assistants or even willing parents.

Where pupils are working creatively, consider carefully whether you are asking them to be creative with language or creative with ICT. The search for the perfect Clip Art or best font/background colour combination has been known to last an entire MFL period! It is perhaps advisable to lay down the simple rule that text be finalised during the lesson where there is access to MFL support resources (including you!) and presentation enhancements should be done for homework, at school or at home. Another approach is to provide an electronic template for pupils to work to, whether it be a series of PowerPoint slides or a writing frame in MS Publisher, for example. Again, customising or further enhancing the presentation should be done out of lesson time.

While the school network team is likely to be responsible for upholding health and safety regulations in the design and maintenance of the ICT suites, it is important to be aware of issues yourself. Make sure you have read your school ICT policy – the BECTA website and InfoTech 5: *Putting achievement first* (Buckland 2000) are also useful sources of guidance. Care is needed with use of the Internet, in particular, due to the large number of clearly inappropriate websites in existence. Remember that it is possible to work on some Web pages off-line, if saved onto the network before a lesson. Finally, problems with the technology do arise, so do always have a back-up plan in mind!

key points	• Pupils have an entitlement to access ICT in the teaching and learning of MFL
	• ICT can provide simultaneous support for a wider range of learning styles
	• ICT offers new opportunities for pupils to work collaboratively and learn from one another
	• Pupils can develop valuable key skills through the application of ICT to MFL
	• Good planning for the use of ICT is essential to ensure that departments, teachers and pupils make the most of their time

Learning to learn
with ICT

chapter 2

☐ How can we support KS3 pupils in learning to learn?

☐ How can the development of language-learning strategies be enhanced by the use of ICT?

☐ What kind of strategies can support independent language learning?

☐ Can ICT help pupils to develop thinking skills which will enable them to learn more effectively?

How can we support KS3 pupils in learning to learn?

This chapter is concerned with the development of language-learning strategies, thinking skills and research skills, which we include under the umbrella term 'study skills'. Our intention is to indicate ways in which pupils can use ICT to help them develop such skills to enable them to become organised, constructive and independent language learners. Chapter 3 then deals with activities which are likely to promote actual language learning in terms of knowledge, understanding and use of the target language. There is a direct link between the two chapters in that pupils should always be reminded of the appropriate study skills and language-learning strategies discussed here when working on the activities.

We are very much concerned in this book with the ways in which ICT can activate the kind of cognitive processes which are likely to promote learning and, thereby, to raise levels of achievement. These processes are effectively sub-conscious activities within the brain which involve:

- storing of new information as knowledge in long-term memory;
- associating incoming information with existing knowledge;
- creating and storing new knowledge by combining new information with existing knowledge;
- retrieving knowledge from long-term memory fluently (speed of retrieval) and accurately (appropriate in meaning and form).

One of the clear messages in the Key Stage 3 Strategy is that such processes are triggered by setting challenging activities, rather than those which tend to be overtly repetitive and to make low level demands on pupils. For example, in the early stages of language learning, asking pupils to generate new sentences from a model, even with only minimal changes to the model, presents a better learning experience than simply copywriting. This is because in addition to copying words correctly, there is a requirement on the learner to understand the meaning of the model and the function within the sentence of the word to be replaced. The learner also has to consider possible replacements, select the most appropriate and spell it correctly. The setting of challenging activities underlies all that follows in this and subsequent chapters.

How can the development of language-learning strategies be enhanced by the use of ICT?

Characteristic behaviours of the successful language learner

Researchers such as Rubin (1975 and 1981) and Stern (1975) identified the kind of behaviours which appear to characterise successful language learners although the learners studied had not been trained in them. The following are adapted from Rubin (1981):

- *seeking clarification;*
- *checking pronunciation, vocabulary, spelling, grammar and style;*
- *adopting various memorisation strategies such as note taking, saying words aloud, making word associations, writing out new vocabulary several times;*
- *guessing at meanings from clues such as key words in a sentence, syntactic structure, pictures, gestures;*
- *using rules to get at meaning;*
- *practising by, for example, experimenting with the pronunciation of new words, talking to yourself in TL, drilling yourself on words in different forms;*
- *creating opportunities to practise, such as contact with native speakers;*
- *using productive tricks such as paraphrase, synonyms, cognates.*

These strategies should be taught explicitly to pupils to enable all to become better and conscious language learners. Whole-class starters and plenaries are very good contexts in which to do so. In addition, these appropriate cognitive processes are more likely to occur if pupils are taught the kind of study skills which will activate them, such as preparing adequately for a task, drafting, reviewing work, self-assessing and using feedback creatively, either from a computer program or from the teacher. The examples in this chapter are suggested ways in which ICT can help to train all pupils to become better learners through the application of the strategies and skills referred to above. They focus on those aspects which can be successfully promoted by the use of ICT. Not all can.

The role of ICT

In looking at the role of ICT in the development of language-learning strategies, we concentrate on the exploitation of three important facilities offered by ICT which differentiate it from more traditional media, namely:

- flexible text;
- immediate feedback;
- ease and speed of data processing and transfer.

The cognitive processes involved in working on a computer are different from those which make use of pen and paper or a blackboard. In the context of study skills, the ability to make changes in computer-generated text without leaving any trace of previous errors or misunderstandings enables learners to:

- draft;
- evaluate;
- revise.

The use of these three skills promotes cognitive activity involving complex linguistic processing which is likely to reinforce correct grammar, syntax and choice of vocabulary because of the level of cognitive activity engendered.

In terms of the feedback facilities offered by some MFL software packages, gap-fill exercises provide a simple but helpful example. The learner types in the word which he or she thinks is appropriate. If the spelling is incorrect, the computer will immediately provide feedback either by signalling that the input is correct, or by retaining any letters which are in the correct position in the answer. It is sometimes possible for the teacher to program in the provision of clues as support. Reinforcement of the nature of the error and the subsequent correction is likely to lead to higher levels of retention than with more traditional systems of feedback. The use of feedback to promote specific kinds of language learning is dealt with in detail in Chapter 3.

Finally, ICT differs from traditional media thanks to:

- the ease with which data can be transferred from one software package to another through the use of copy and paste;

- the speed with which computers process data such as with the search and sort facilities provided by database packages;
- the ability of computers to produce statistical information in graphical format such as bar charts and graphs.

These facilities are very helpful within challenging problem-solving activities such as, for example, the textbook favourite, survey work. In this instance, they relieve pupils of having to do tedious tasks such as writing and photocopying questionnaires, entering data into a card reference system by hand, searching subsequently for matches and drawing graphical representations such as bar charts. As a result, pupils have more time for higher-level activities such as prediction and analysis, which are likely to trigger appropriate cognitive processing.

Combining different ICT applications within an extended activity

While you will find later in this chapter suggestions for using ICT to encourage the use of specific strategies and skills, it is important to bear in mind that a particularly fruitful approach to improving learning efficiency is to set up extended activities lasting several weeks which take advantage of all three ways in which ICT can trigger cognitive processes. ICT is an excellent tool for getting pupils to re-use language in different contexts, something which undoubtedly leads to deep learning.

For example, a Year 8 class is focusing on the construction of complex sentences involving clauses of reason. The grammar work is being done in the context of leisure activities and holidays. They have already worked on the relevant vocabulary and structures over the previous four weeks, including using the *Fun with Texts* text manipulation package which provided them with immediate feedback (described in Chapter 3). The textbook suggests that they put their newly learned language to good use to do a survey to find out the following:

- how many people in their class prefer to go to the seaside, countryside or mountains for their holidays and why;
- whether they prefer to go abroad or to stay in their own country and why;
- how they prefer to travel and why;
- who they prefer to have as their companions and why.

They use a word processor to create their class questionnaire and type an e-mail to send it to their link class. They remember to include a field in their database for the name of the school so that comparisons can be made between the two classes.

They set up a database to help them answer the questions listed above. They type into the database their own responses to their questionnaire and then copy and paste in the responses from the link class sent as attachments to an e-mail message.

Finally, they work in pairs or threes to answer specific questions which they present to the rest of the class, possibly using graphics such as bar charts generated by the computer. They are required always to give the reasons for the preferences indicated by pupils.

The example given above involves group activity. What follows is concerned with the pupil as an independent learner.

What kind of strategies can support independent language learning?

Organising learning

Given the number of subjects in the secondary timetable, it is little wonder that pupils can appear disorganised. While some pupils seem to thrive in the midst of chaos, the majority do not. They need to be systematic about their learning, to know where they are going, to be able to monitor their progress, to understand where they have failed and to know how to put things right.

Simply using the motivational power of ICT to encourage pupils to keep a learning diary by filling in a template is likely to lead to a more disciplined approach to learning. Such a template could take the form of a table within a Word document and involve, for example, target setting (what I plan to do and by when), self-evaluation (to what extent did I achieve my targets, what is my evidence, where do I need to improve?) and action plan (what do I need to do to improve and by when?).

Learning diary

Learning objective?	By when?	How to check my success?	How did I do? 1–5	How can I improve on this?
Endings for adjectives, regular and irregular	10/11	Do Exercise 4, page 21 and check my answers in the grammar section	4	Revise feminine endings of irregular adjectives
Read and understand poem page 24 with help of dictionary	14/10	Amount of poem understood before lesson	3	Go back over poem at home after explanations in lesson
Revise pronunciation of new words from today's lesson	18/10	Use words without correction in next lesson	5	All OK!
Revise form of irregular verbs incorrect in last homework	21/10	Get all my corrections right		

This kind of technique could also be used to help pupils to collect together new language items under appropriate headings, with encouragement for them to comment on the items in order to improve their chances of internalising them. They can use the 'Find' facility in Word to search for the item that they want when drafting or checking work. In this way, they can build up their own searchable language reference tool. These two suggestions require regular access to a computer lab, or out-of-school access to the school network. If this is possible the documents can be kept on the network. If pupils are unable to access the school network from home, but have an e-mail account at home and at school, they can transfer their diary and reference tool between home and school as an attachment to an e-mail message. Such diaries and reference tools can be seen as part of the learning process and, as such, assessed regularly by the teacher, or kept as entirely private documents. If properly kept they underline progress for pupils and show how the various components of their learning link together.

From a technical point of view, care needs to be taken in setting up learning diaries, or any other documents which are intended for long-term use by children at home and at school. The use of floppy discs for data transfer is not allowed by many schools because of the risk of viruses and the A drives are often disenabled. You also need to be aware that it is the practice in some schools to delete pupil files on a regular basis. In order to enable pupils to keep diaries, you need to negotiate permanent space for them on the network server.

Memorising

There are many ways of memorising, such as the use of songs, mnemonics, visual associations, word associations and the learning of poems, for example, by heart, some of which you no doubt use already. None of these necessarily make use of ICT. However, when it comes to vocabulary, there are packages specifically designed to help pupils to learn new words. The *Vocab* program within the *Authoring Suite* from WIDA Software is particularly helpful in that it enables pupils to build up their own vocabulary lists, including example sentences containing the target items. Once a list has been entered, the computer sets up six games using the list as the content. The games include word order in sentences, anagrams, putting words in alphabetical order, hangman using sentences, multiple choice and a WIDA special called *Mindword*. Pupils receive scores which they seem to enjoy trying to improve. Lists can be saved over the course of a year and provide an excellent revision tool. You can see a demo of *Vocab* on the WIDA site.

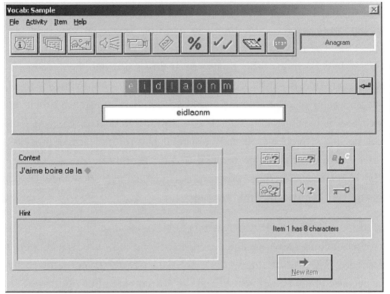

Source: *Vocab* from the *Authoring Suite* (WIDA Software)

Wordlearn from BrainSystems is a comparative newcomer to the market and can be downloaded from the Web. It is much more limited than *Vocab* and does not have the facility to include sentences. However, it is shareware and therefore cheaper. Remember that shareware is not 'free' ware! You usually download it from the Web and are able to use it for a trial period before buying it. For example, with *Wordlearn*, you get a 30 day trial period after which you have to register your copy and pay a modest registration fee in order to continue using it.

The facility for continual repetition which ICT offers promotes memorising informally, because pupils seem to engage with the vocabulary list or text in a way that they do not using other media. It is not unknown for Key Stage 3 pupils to spend a full 50 minute lesson working on the same text within the *Fun with Texts* package (see Chapter 3) and to be able to recall the vocabulary and structures learned during the experience quickly and accurately several months later. Teachers have also reported successful outcomes from the use of course-related old favourites such as

En Route and *Unterwegs* from Granada Learning as well as from the recently published *Métro Electro* from Heinemann.

Experimentation in a supportive environment

Successful language learners tend to be risk takers. They are willing to experiment and seem able to cope when the experimentation proves wrong. A word processor offers a comparatively safe environment in that errors can be easily corrected and can therefore be helpful in developing a positive attitude towards writing. It is possible to make it even more 'pupil-friendly' if differentiated 'help' documents are made available as files on the network by the teacher when appropriate. For example, if pupils are composing text, the most able might only require some hints, rather than suggested vocabulary and structures. For the middle ability band, it might be useful to provide them with some vocabulary and suggested structures. For those pupils likely to experience real difficulties, a help file could contain template sentences, which they could copy and paste in their document and then modify. The kind of text manipulation packages described in Chapter 3 are even 'safer' environments in which to experiment and take risks because ultimately, it is possible to succeed, even if it means a somewhat reduced score.

The most challenging of the activities offered by text manipulation is total text reconstruction (the *Copywrite* program in *Fun with Texts* from Camsoft and *Storyboard* from WIDA). This activity involves the teacher typing or pasting in a short text and the computer then replacing every letter in the text by a dash or asterisk. The pupils have to type in whole words which they believe to be in the text. Any instance of the word in the text will appear in its rightful place and if the word is not in the text, the feedback simply tells the pupil this. It is an activity which certainly encourages experimentation. However, it can be refined and rendered even more beneficial if pupils are given some ideas of how to go about their experimentation and are required to work with a text on a topic and vocabulary base of which they have some experience.

Their first sub-strategy might therefore be to try out likely nouns. When their input is rejected, they could check the form of the noun that they used and, if that doesn't work, they could possibly try to find a synonym if their linguistic knowledge extends that far. When they have exhausted their fund of likely nouns, they could try out high frequency words. These will give them a framework within which to begin to predict the class of word needed to fill the gaps that remain and its form. When they have tried out all their relevant linguistic knowledge, they can always 'buy' the words necessary to complete the text, at the cost of a few points off their score. You might find it interesting to observe pupils engaged in text reconstruction. It can be quite revealing of their use of strategy, level of linguistic knowledge and lack of understanding in surprising areas!

Making opportunities to interact with native speakers

This is yet another strategy used by successful language learners. Contact with native speakers in whatever form is useful for providing cultural insights, reading 'real' language and writing for a 'real' audience. It helps to develop fluency rather than accuracy. There are various communication technologies available to us, such as e-mail, which open up opportunities for interaction likely to prepare pupils for coping with face-to-face meetings in the future. The example given below of participation in a bulletin board or forum is another way of encouraging the more reluctant learners to make use of this strategy, even if only passively in some instances.

A bulletin board or forum is a structured on-line discussion based on a central theme and organised into sub-themes. Participants can merely read the input of others or respond to that input by contributing their own views. Contributions can be prepared off-line and then posted up on-line. Extreme care should be taken by language teachers to investigate carefully public bulletin boards and forums before encouraging pupils to participate. Pupils should also be told never to reveal their real name, gender or location when communicating with strangers on-line. The possibilities offered by bulletin boards and e-mail and the security issues involved are discussed fully in InfoTech 7: *Communicating on-line* (Gläsmann 2004).

The best kind of bulletin board for younger pupils is perhaps one set up by the teacher, possibly in collaboration with the teacher of a link class. Also worth looking at are target-language websites designed specifically for children which host on-line discussions on given topics. Readers of the website send in views on the topic under discussion, which might be 'The World of Sport', for example. They do this simply by logging on to the website, going to the appropriate area and following the instructions for posting messages. Contributions consist either of a response to a point already made or the introduction of a new sub-topic. While all contributions are checked by website personnel before they are made public, it is still advisable to monitor such sites very closely yourself. Mômes.net (French) and Kindernetz (German) are popular examples offering regular opportunities for participation (see Kindernetz example on p32).

Given the public nature of the activity, participating in a bulletin board involves a degree of risk-taking far greater than the controlled environments of the word processor or text manipulation package discussed earlier. Pupils could therefore progress from these safer environments to a more public arena when they are ready.

Repetition to improve oral performance

The value of sub-conscious repetition in the context of extended exposure to texts has been discussed above. Conscious repetition of the spoken language within a multimedia context is helpful in terms of relating sound to spelling, improving pronunciation and intonation and practising complete sentences within a recorded dialogue. The precision, ease and speed with which recordings made on a CD-ROM can be played back makes the experience of repetition more attractive to pupils. This is especially true if pupils have been trained in sound discrimination to enable them to assess their own input against that of the native speaker model and make any necessary changes. Words can also be shown on screen simultaneously to support the oral work. Most course-related CD-ROMs provide record and playback facilities, as do multilingual packages such as *Smart Start* (formerly *Triple Play Plus*), available from Camsoft.

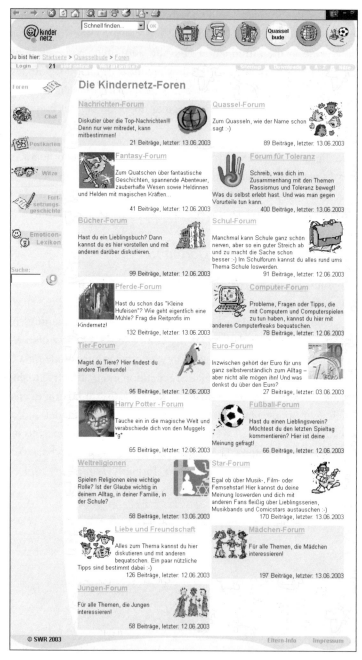

Can ICT help pupils to develop thinking skills which will enable them to learn more effectively?

The promotion of thinking skills is an intrinsic part of the Government's Key Stage 3 Strategy and they have been the subject of research over many years. They are conducive to successful language learning provided that they are taught, practised and their use monitored. Unlike several of the language-learning strategies discussed above, thinking skills are generic.

There are many views of what thinking skills actually are. The best known is the cognitive component of a broader taxonomy of behaviours important to learning which was drawn up by Bloom (1956) and his associates. The original version also includes affective and psycho-motor behaviours. On p34 you will find an adaptation of the cognitive domain which consists of a hierarchy of six levels. The most complex level is no. 1 and is at the top of the list. The levels are concerned with the complexity of the behaviours. They are not dependent on the age of the learner or, in the case of MFL, on the learner's degree of competence in the target language. Bloom's levels have no connection with National Curriculum levels!

The exemplar actions are not part of the original taxonomy. They are illustrative of the kind of actions that pupils need to take in problem-solving tasks, which are excellent vehicles for the promotion of the skills. You will no doubt be able to add other actions which you believe are appropriate in the MFL setting and the key is to make sure that pupils are aware of the skills they are applying in a given task.

A good example of an MFL activity likely to promote more complex cognitive processing is as follows. Instead of asking pupils to read a short text about a particular soft drink to extract specific details, you ask them to read two texts in order to compare one soft drink with another. Here, a much broader range of thinking skills comes into play including analysis, evaluation and judgment. Greater engagement with the text leads to deeper and more lasting learning.

Problem-solving tasks are an excellent way of promoting thinking skills. They can be of any length. They can, for example, involve something as quick as finding as many adjectives of colour within a Word document as quickly as possible and listing them in alphabetical order, possibly in the masculine singular form for those able to

Level	Cognitive behaviour	Examples of relevant actions

Level ▼   **Cognitive behaviour** ▼   **Examples of relevant actions** ▼

1 — **Evaluation**
- assessing
- judging
- selecting from a number of alternatives
- rating
- recommending

2 — **Synthesis**
- combining information from various sources
- inferring and deducing
- conjecturing based on incoming information
- generalising
- drawing conclusions

3 — **Analysis**
- analysing
- appraising
- comparing and contrasting
- experimenting
- discriminating

4 — **Application**
- using existing knowledge in a new context
- applying known rules
- dramatising
- illustrating
- interpreting

5 — **Comprehension**
- classifying
- describing
- explaining
- locating
- restating

6 — **Knowledge**
- recognising
- recalling
- labelling/naming
- repeating/copying
- duplicating

'deconstruct' feminine and plural forms. Rather than reading through the text and recognising the words, pupils are told to use the 'Find' facility in Word to predict and locate words (go to Edit > Find); then 'copy' and 'paste' and finally the 'Sort' facility (located in the Table menu) to make them into an alphabetical list without the need for copy writing.

This seemingly trivial task is enhanced by the use of ICT since it raises the level of the thinking skills involved in identifying the adjectives from 'recognising' (level 6) to 'experimenting' (level 3), although 'recalling' (level 6) would be used to initiate the search process. Pupils would also have to use 'applying rules' (level 4) to identify adjectives describing feminine and plural nouns and 'assessing' (level 1), if a word that they tried out was not found. When it comes to making up the list, they would be freed from having to engage in 'copying' (level 6). For the more able, there would be an additional activity at level 3 concerned with 'analysing' the form of each of the words and at level 2, 'drawing conclusions' about the masculine form of the adjective based on their own knowledge and the number and gender of the noun qualified by the adjective in question.

In setting up problem-solving tasks involving ICT, the trick is to spot ways in which ICT can relieve pupils of activities which involve low-level skills (e.g. electronic copying and pasting, rather than copying out by hand) and in which it can provoke the use of higher-level skills. It is also important to suggest appropriate strategies to pupils. For example, they may not know that they can search for parts of words or whole words and that, in the example above, the most efficient way to search initially is by using the masculine singular form of the adjective, although additional searches will be necessary where the feminine and/or plural form differs considerably, as for example in the case of *beau/belle*.

Now that you are familiar with some of the actions contained with Bloom's taxonomy of thinking skills or behaviours, you might like to return to the extended Year 8 task combining different ICT applications described on p24 and list by level and skill category the number of actions that you can detect in the tasks set. When you have done that, you might like to consider some of the activities described in your textbook to assess the level of demand made on pupils, and how you might increase the challenge and diminish the drudgery by the introduction of ICT.

Research techniques

Research techniques gain their place as a sub-set of study skills for language learning now that access to TL resources on the Web is commonplace. Research techniques in an ICT context involve the following:

- locating information by using a search engine;
- evaluating information in terms of, for example, reliability, accuracy, relevance, topicality;
- re-purposing information in order to, for example, present it to others.

The three research techniques listed above are part of the 'learning to learn' process in that, if used correctly, they provide pupils with the means to access content in the TL which is an essential component in current language-learning practices at Key Stage 3. Equally importantly, in order for pupils to use research techniques effectively, they need to bring into play a wide range of higher-level thinking skills to help them to find wholly relevant materials.

Searching and evaluating

In order to use a search engine well, pupils need to be able to identify key words which will help them to locate information relevant to the subject of their research. Once they have located a potential text, they need first of all to evaluate its accessibility in terms of their own level of competence in the target language before evaluating it in terms listed above. At Key Stage 3, care has to be taken to ensure that pupils access sites which offer texts of a suitable linguistic level and length and it might well be that they are given leads to follow up by way of URLs, rather than let loose on search engines. Search engines can be dangerous tools at any age if a firewall is not in place and care should be taken in setting out-of-school work involving the use of search engines.

Re-purposing information

If pupils are required to present the fruits of their research to the rest of the class, they might well have to 're-purpose' it. For example, if their task is to report back on the leisure facilities of a town in a country where the TL is spoken, they might well find a website which contains the information, but it is unlikely that it will be in a suitable format. If pupils are not to waste their time copying off the screen by hand, they need to employ their existing skills to copy and paste text and, if appropriate, graphics into a Word document where they can be edited. If the presentation is to take the form of a written document for display on the wall, layout will be all important. If, on the other hand, the information is to be delivered orally, pupils will find it helpful to use PowerPoint slides if a computer + projector + screen/interactive whiteboard are available.

key points	• Pupils who are conscious of why, what and how they are to learn are more likely to raise their levels of achievement
	• In order to become conscious learners pupils need to be taught to apply thinking skills in an explicit way. MFL teachers need to capitalise on work done in this regard in the primary school and in other departments in their own school
	• Language-learning strategies are a vital component of study skills and they, too, need to be taught. Starters and plenaries are good contexts in which to do so
	• If pupils are motivated to make individual contact with the target culture via the wealth of opportunities offered by the Internet, they will benefit so much more if they have well-developed research and coping strategies, including how to re-purpose information
	• ICT offers significant opportunities for supporting the development of study skills likely to lead to successful independent learning

Promoting knowledge and use of the target language with ICT

chapter 3

☐ How can KS3 pupils acquire knowledge and understanding of the target language and an ability to use it successfully with ICT?

☐ Can word-processing and text-manipulation functions promote cognitive processes leading to deeper and longer-lasting learning?

☐ What kind of ICT solutions will meet pupil needs at word, sentence and text level?

How can KS3 pupils acquire knowledge and understanding of the target language and an ability to use it successfully with ICT?

One of the more challenging aspects of the revised Programme of Study in the National Curriculum for MFL is the direct reference to the need for pupils to gain knowledge of the grammar of the target language, including the link between the spoken and written word, and of how to apply that knowledge in order to express themselves. The Key Stage 3 MFL Framework promotes greater focus on the form of the language at word, sentence and text level, and you will find suggestions for activities which deal with specific aspects of language at each of the three language levels later in this chapter. All seek to exploit the facilities offered by ICT that are more likely than traditional media to lead to deep and lasting learning in the context of knowledge, understanding and use of the target language.

Moving from the establishment of meaning to the creation of meaningful language

This chapter focuses on ICT activities based on word processing and text manipulation, using the written word as a tool for learning. They should all enable pupils to fulfil the requirements of the Programme of Study in respect of knowledge of the target language and its practical application in all four skill areas. The suggested activities build on the knowledge about language which pupils have already acquired in primary school and ongoing literacy development at Key Stage 3. They address the progression which begins with the introduction of a grammatical concept, leads on to a recognition of its role in the creation of meaning and ends in its productive use in the generation of new chunks of language at an appropriate level by individual pupils. Above all, the activities seek to exploit the dynamic features of computer-based text, in that words, sentences and chunks of text can be moved around a screen, can be changed in response to a variety of stimuli and are provisional until the pupil decides that they are final. Suggestions are also made for bridging the gap between reading and writing, between the establishment of meaning in existing texts through reading and the creation of new meaning in personal statements and questions.

One of the problems associated with writing using pen and paper is that the less well-motivated the pupil, the less likely they are to make an initial stab at a challenging activity, reflect on the quality of their input and write out a revised version. However, as indicated in Chapter 2, these are the very processes which engage pupils cognitively and which, as a result, tend to lead to increased levels of achievement. Activities based on computer-generated text are willingly engaged in by most pupils, however, even though they are often more challenging than a similar paper-based version. By 'having a stab' at an activity, pupils are effectively risk taking.

Can word-processing and text-manipulation functions promote cognitive processes leading to deeper and longer-lasting learning?

Functions provided by a word processor

While its primary purpose is to compose and produce a written document, in language-learning terms a word processor is a remarkable tool for the creation of stimulating and interactive electronic worksheets which can include text, graphics and sound in various combinations. The appropriate use of the facilities described below will enable you to set up a wide range of activities, directly linked to the Scheme of Work, and differentiated according to the needs of individual groups of pupils.

Word-processing function ▼	Function exploited in MFL context ▼
Dragging and dropping	Pupils highlight a word from an assorted list of words, 'drag' it to the appropriate word class box and 'drop' it in.
Expanding a text (insertion)	Pupils insert adjectives, adverbs and phrases to enhance an existing text.
Reducing a text (deletion)	Pupils delete unnecessary words from a text to reduce it to the bare bones.

Editing a text (insertion and deletion)	Pupils make step-by-step changes to given words in a sentence to transform its meaning.
Re-ordering a text (copy/cut and paste)	Pupils put a jumbled set of instructions into the correct order.
Editing a text in response to a graphic	Pupils expand a text to reflect what they see in the graphic within the electronic worksheet.
Editing a text in response to a recorded text	Pupils click on the sound file icon within their electronic worksheet, listen to a recording of the text and type in missing words in the written text.
Highlighting and colouring text	Pupils go through a text highlighting different classes of words according to an agreed colour scheme.

Remember that automatic correction and/or feedback is not possible within a word-processed document, unlike with text-manipulation software as described on p43. If you plan to mark your pupils' work, you can either get them to print it out, save it in the Homework area on the network or send it to you as an e-mail attachment if they have e-mail accounts on the school system. You can then choose to print work out for marking or mark it electronically using the Insert Comment feature in Word. Alternatively, you can encourage pupils to assess their own work when completed by checking it against an 'answer file'. At the end of this chapter you will find a variety of worked activities which exploit word-processing functions across word, sentence and text level.

Developing writing skills

In addition to their exciting potential in electronic worksheets, these word-processing functions are also of great value to pupils as writers. The following are the processes that pupils should be advised to go through when composing a text using a word processor if they are to develop their linguistic skills rather than simply produce a fair copy:

- drafting to get ideas down;
- reviewing to check content, choice of vocabulary, spelling and grammar;
- editing to reflect the results of the review;
- revising to make sure that changes made at the editing stage have not introduced further errors;
- second editing to ensure that sentences are correctly formed and that all spellings are correct.

Optional skills:
- dictionary skills;
- using a target language spelling and grammar checker, provided that prior training has been given.

The use of word processors simply to produce a fair copy is unproductive in language-learning terms and can lead to the reinforcement of existing errors and the creation of new ones. The purpose of composition using a word processor is to enable pupils to expand their effective use of the TL through taking risks with new language and by bringing specific linguistic items into active use and to combine them actively with existing linguistic knowledge. The editing facilities provided within a word processor are also available in PowerPoint and will promote the same cognitive processes.

Functions provided by text-manipulation packages

Text-manipulation packages provide facilities for teachers to create texts around which a variety of interactive activities are automatically generated by the software. In all text-manipulation packages it is possible to copy and paste text from other electronic documents including Web pages. Activities can be closely tied to the Scheme of Work and to the needs of pupils with differing levels of ability. All of the packages referred to in this chapter can be networked, provided that the appropriate licence has been purchased. You can try them out by visiting the relevant websites, where you will also find details of prices and suggestions for the curricular use of the packages. The types of interaction offered by each package are summarised in the grid on p45. The following are the packages referred to in this chapter:

Fun with Texts	Camsoft	www.camsoftpartners.co.uk

This software offers eight types of interactive activity. It can be installed on individual computers or on a network, depending on the hardware configuration that you have available to your department. Libraries of files can be built up for future use.

The Authoring Suite	WIDA software	www.wida.co.uk/auth

The full *Authoring Suite* consists of six types of interactive activity. It also includes programs for setting up multiple-choice tasks and tests requiring free text entry answers, as well as an activity to identify the title of a text from a version of the text with very few words showing. A vocabulary-building activity is also being updated (Spring 2003). It is possible to have a cut-down version of the package consisting of your own choice of programs. As with *Fun with Texts,* libraries of files can be built up for future use. The software has the facility to provide an introduction to an activity with suggested strategies and helpful hints, and it is also possible to provide a glossary. Both of these facilities are very useful when setting up self-access activities. The software can be used on individual computers or on a network.

Gapkit	Camsoft	www.camsoftpartners.co.uk

This provides more extensive gap-creating facilities than those available in *Fun with Texts,* and includes a multiple-choice option. The software can be used on individual computers or on a network.

Hot Potatoes	University of Victoria, Canada	www.uvic.ca/hrd/halfbaked

The *Hot Potatoes* suite includes six types of interactive activity for use on the World Wide Web. In effect this means that activities are created on the computer on which the software is installed, but that pupils can log on to the Web and work on the activities on any computer, whether in school or not. This software can be downloaded from the website and is free to non-profit educational users who make their activities available to others on the Web. If you do not want to offer your activities to others, a licensing fee is payable.

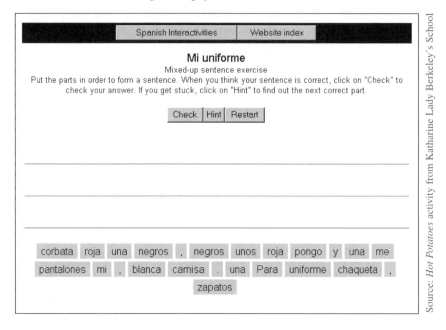

Source: *Hot Potatoes* activity from Katharine Lady Berkeley's School

Multimedia facilities are currently available in *Gapkit, The Authoring Suite* and *Hot Potatoes.* They will be available in *Fun with Texts* by 2004. It is therefore possible to enhance some of the activities described on pp48–52 at word level, in that a complete version of the text could be recorded.

Pupils can then click on the sound icon to hear the text, identify the word that they need and work out how to spell it from its sound. It is also possible to complete activities in a whole-class setting with the teacher providing spoken commentary, where sound recordings are not available.

The table below summarises lists the types of activity provided by each of the packages:

	Fun with Texts	Gapkit	The Authoring Suite	Hot Potatoes
Type of activity				
Multimedia facilities	By 2004	•	•	•
Gap filling	•	•	•	•
Cloze procedure	•	•	•	
Text reconstruction by multiple choice	•			
Partial text reconstruction	•		•	
Complete text reconstruction	•		•	
Re-ordering text	•		•	•
Unscrambling words	•			
Decoding words	•			
Matching			•	•

The text-manipulation activities at word, sentence and/or text level featured on p46 promote similar cognitive processes to those involved in word processing but are enhanced by the provision of feedback. Feedback on an incorrect attempt usually consists of a clue rather than provision of the correct answer, further activating these processes by sending pupils back inside their heads to identify what is wrong. When pupils have exhausted all the possibilities provided by the clues, they can ask for the correct answer. In addition, because it is possible to use the same text with a number of different types of interaction, the activities encourage pupils to work with the same text several times, albeit in different ways. This has the result of reinforcing the vocabulary and structures contained in the text to the extent that pupils are often able to reproduce both without having formally 'learned' them.

A closer look at functions, interactions and strategies

Type of activity	Nature of interaction	Level of operation	Form of feedback
Gap filling	Completing gaps consisting of parts of words, full words and phrases	Word, sentence or text	Letters in the correct locations within the word are retained, along with written, spoken or visual clues
Cloze procedure	Filling in every 'nth' word	Sentence or text	Incorrect words not put into text
Text reconstruction by multiple choice	Selection of the correct word from list	Sentence	If incorrect word is chosen, it is not shown in the developing text
Full or partial text reconstruction by pupil input	Typing in words likely to appear in the text	Essentially text level, but to some extent at word and sentence level, too	If incorrect word is chosen, it is not shown in the developing text
Re-ordering text	Moving around jumbled lines of text until in the correct order	Word, sentence or text level	The exchange of lines does not take place if incorrect
Unscrambling words within a text	Highlighting a word and typing in the correct spelling	Word, but also sentence	Incorrect words are not displayed
Decoding words within a text	Deciding how each letter of the alphabet has been encoded (e.g. e = j)	Word	Letters are not changed in the text if the decoding is incorrect
Matching	Deciding which chunk of language in one column matches with a chunk of language in the second column	Word, sentence or text	If incorrect text is chosen, 'no match' is displayed

In each of the above activities, the principal cognitive activities are:

• prediction based on prior linguistic and/or world knowledge or context;
• linguistic processing of many kinds in response to feedback.

Risk taking is often required, although within a safe environment which is success-orientated.

The more challenging the activity, the more learning will take place. However, since all the texts on which the activities are based are electronic and under the control of the teacher, differentiation is always possible. The use of texts which pupils have been asked to memorise rarely leads to lasting learning as the texts become, in effect, tests of short-term memory and involve little cognitive activity.

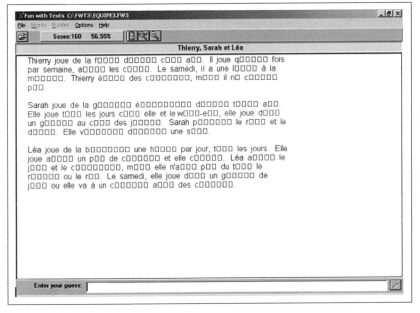

Source: *Copywrite* exercise from *Fun with Texts*

Some of the types of interaction offered by text-manipulation packages above, along with the various word-processing functions, are of more value than others. This is reflected in the frequency with which they are used in the suggestions for activities given in the sections below.

What kind of ICT solutions will meet pupil needs at word, sentence and text level?

Dealing with words

Words have three essential properties – they have at least one meaning, an individual sound and their own spelling. In many languages, nouns are also likely to have a gender, which is a difficult concept for those for whom gender is absent in their mother tongue.

Pupils need to learn to link sounds and spelling successfully as well as to learn to pronounce words correctly, since bad pronunciation is a great barrier to meaning for the listener. ICT provides excellent opportunities for dealing with both of these problem areas provided that multimedia computers with headsets are available. The software to produce the necessary sound files is likely to be available on all multimedia computers in your school and should be comparatively easy to use. Sound files can be inserted into word-processed documents, by going to Insert > Object/Sound file or Insert > Hyperlink.

Some words have different forms according to the function that they perform within a sentence, which poses problems for pupils whose mother tongue has few inflections. For example, 'the' has three different forms according to its function in relation to nouns in the following sentence: *Voici la règle, le crayon et les feuilles de papier.*

High-frequency words are often 'little' (e.g. and, but, who, because) but they are often more essential to the establishment of meaning than bigger words. However, they are difficult to learn because they are often 'connectives' of one kind or another and, as such, do not have the potential visual or sensory links which concrete nouns and 'action' verbs have. Equally they cannot be 'clustered' as readily as can nouns, verbs, adverbs and adjectives.

The activities which follow aim to develop pupils' understanding and strategies for working at word level. Productive use of words such as prepositions, pronouns, adverbs of time, relative adjectives and adverbs, and interrogatives are dealt with in 'Working at sentence level' on p52.

Linking sound and spelling

Activity	Pupils listen to a recording of individual words, identify their written form from a pool of words in a box in a word-processed document and then drag and drop them into their correct position in a list which matches the order in which the words are spoken. This can be followed up by typing out the words as they are spoken.
Teaching intention	To link sound with spelling receptively and actively
Setting	Computer lab – multimedia computers + headsets required
Software required	Sound recording software + Media Player (part of Windows) + word processor

Getting the pronunciation right

Activity	Pupils listen to an appropriate digitally recorded text containing a word list and record their input by repeating what they have heard. They then listen to the recording and use the strategies they have been taught to assess their input and to make changes in their pronunciation where necessary.
Teaching intention	Accuracy of pronunciation of individual words based on a model
Setting	Computer lab – multimedia computers + headsets required
Software required	Sound recording software + Media Player (part of Windows) + word processor if pupils are to have a written list of the words

Learning the gender of words

Activity	Pupils begin with a text containing a number of nouns which are highlighted in colour – red for feminine and blue for masculine. They then insert the correct article. This is followed up by a second text in which the articles are present, but into which pupils drag and drop nouns from a box beneath the text.
Teaching intention	To reinforce the knowledge of the gender of a series of nouns recently taught
Setting	Computer lab
Software required	Word processor

Inflections

Activity	Pupils complete a gap-filling activity where the ends of the verbs have been deleted. The text describes what different people do in their leisure time, including the author of the text. They then work with the same text in another activity, to unscramble each word, including the verbs, again looking carefully at the subject of the verb.
Teaching intention	To focus on inflections and the relationship between subject and verb endings
Setting	A computer lab or a classroom with a computer + projector and screen or interactive whiteboard. This activity can be run in whole-class mode, or partly in full-class mode and partly as independent or small-group work using the networked computers.
Software required	*Cloze* (in which the teacher can specify the gaps) and *Scrambler* from *Fun with Texts*

Learning the 'little' words

Activity	Pupils begin by matching up halves of sentences, the first half of which ends with a preposition. The sentences make up a text which relates to a picture provided as support. They next complete a gap-filling exercise with gaps for prepositions, using the same text or another that describes the picture. There are differentiated versions of the text, one with a box containing the prepositions to be used, the other without. Pupils either drag and drop the words or type them in, according to their ability.
Teaching intention	Reinforcement of recognition and use of previously taught prepositions
Setting	Computer lab
Software required	Matching software + word processor or gap-filling package

Word clusters

Activity	Pupils, working in pairs, open a file which contains a number of similar word clusters (e.g. *penseur, pensif, pensivement, penser* – noun, adjective, adverb, verb). They are given twenty minutes to drag the words in the word clusters to word class boxes. They then spend five minutes discussing the kinds of endings which are characteristic of the different word classes and their findings are then discussed in a whole-class plenary. Dictionaries can be used if appropriate training has been given.
Teaching intention	To enable pupils to 'discover' the characteristic endings for different word classes as an aid to reading for detailed meaning

Setting	Computer lab with facilities to talk meaningfully with a whole class while using a computer, projector and screen or whiteboard
Software required	Word processor

Working at sentence level

Sentences consist of words, the order and form of which is determined by the grammar and syntax of the language in question. The word order might be different from that used in the pupil's mother tongue and this might cause problems in decoding sentences. The decoding problem is increased when pupils begin to encounter compound and complex sentences.

A knowledge of grammar and syntax is essential both as a way of understanding the meaning of sentences and of composing meaningful sentences. It is important for pupils to realise that grammar is not simply a matter of rules, but that without it, there would be little or no meaning within either spoken or written language. They need to appreciate that all languages have grammatical patterns and that, for the most part, such patterns are regular.

Sentences are either statements or questions, and statements can be either positive or negative. Pupils need to able to differentiate between sentence types both in terms of word order and the use in context of many of the 'little' words discussed earlier. Pupils can experiment with word order by transforming sentences from and into statements, negatives and questions, thereby applying their knowledge of grammar in preparation for generating their own sentences.

Word order

Activity	Pupils unscramble jumbled-up sentences based on a given structure. They then complete a word-processing activity in which they are given a list of words – they have either to type them into sentences or drag and drop them into place. These sentences are based on the same sentence structure featured in the unscrambling activity. These two activities

are particularly successful in German, but can be used in Romance languages with regard to the position of adjectives and negative sentences and questions.

Teaching intention	To provide reinforcement of previously taught sentence structure through recognition and sentence generation
Setting	Computer lab
Software required	Software which offers un-jumbling of sentences + word processor

Pattern recognition

Activity	Pupils work with software which enables them to build up a text prepared by the teacher using multiple choice. The text is composed of sentences which each follow the same pattern (e.g. perfect tense verbs in French in a given person). They then work on the same text in which the subject and the verbs have been blanked out. They reconstruct the text by typing in the words which they think are missing.
Teaching intention	To enable pupils to demonstrate recognition of a pattern and to apply their knowledge of the pattern
Setting	Computer lab or as a full-class activity in a classroom with projection facilities
Software required	*Prediction* and *Copywrite* (text reconstruction) in *Fun with Texts*

Transformation

Activity	The teacher presents a sentence within a word-processed document to pupils using the classroom computer and projection facilities. He or she then asks the pupils to suggest how to change a given word in order to alter the

meaning of the sentence. The class of the word is discussed and possible replacements are suggested. A vote is taken on the most appropriate, based on criteria such as meaning, target language usage and correctness of form. This process continues, possibly including insertions and deletions, until the sentence has been completely transformed. It has to make good sense at each stage.

Teaching intention	To revise particular points at the end of a unit of work in a holistic rather than an isolated way and to stimulate pupils to connect the various items of new knowledge with themselves and with existing knowledge
Setting	Classroom with computer and projection facilities
Software required	Word processor

Example of transformation activity

<u>Tomorrow</u> afternoon Peter is leaving home to spend a week with his grandparents.

<u>This</u> afternoon Peter is leaving home to spend a week with his grandparents.

This afternoon Peter is leaving home to spend <u>a week</u> with his grandparents.

This afternoon Peter is leaving home to spend <u>the weekend</u> with his grandparents.

This afternoon <u>Peter</u> is leaving home <u>to spend the weekend</u> with his grandparents.

This afternoon <u>my cousin</u> is leaving home to spend the weekend with his grandparents.

This afternoon my cousin is leaving <u>home</u> to spend the weekend with his grandparents.

This afternoon my cousin is leaving <u>London</u> to spend the weekend with his grandparents.

This <u>afternoon</u> my cousin is leaving London to spend the weekend with his grandparents.

This <u>morning</u> my cousin is leaving London to spend the weekend with his grandparents.

This morning my cousin is <u>leaving</u> London to spend the weekend with his uncle.

This morning my cousin is <u>going to</u> London to spend the weekend with his uncle.

This morning my cousin is going to London to spend the weekend with his <u>grandparents</u>.

This morning my cousin is going to London to spend the weekend with his <u>uncle</u>.

This morning my cousin is going to London to <u>spend the weekend</u> with his uncle.

This morning my cousin is going to London to <u>visit a museum</u> with his uncle.

Coping with texts

Clearly pupils need to apply their knowledge about individual words and sentence structure when reading or attempting to compose a longer text. However, more so than at sentence level, they also need knowledge of the form and role of pronouns such as subject, object and relative pronouns, and other connectives. Also as they progress in the target language, they need to develop knowledge of tenses. When reading a text, they need to apply skills such as skimming and scanning to get the gist, but that should be their starting point, not their destination. It is easy to be misled when reading for gist and a detailed reading including an understanding of the 'little' words is essential to get the full meaning, even if pupils still do not understand every word without reference to a glossary, dictionary or the teacher. Different strategies to establish meaning come into play at this point, including using the kind of word knowledge discussed earlier. Writing a short piece of continuous text involves a degree of cohesion which requires more complex techniques than simply producing a series of sentences.

Identifying appropriate pronouns and connectives

Activity	Following a plenary discussion about the different kinds of connectives previously studied, pupils work on the partial reconstruction of a text from which all the connectives (such as pronouns, conjunctions, relative pronouns and adverbs) have been removed. When they have completed the partial reconstruction, they are encouraged to work with the same text again, this time reconstructing it in full. For a class containing a wide ability range, the first activity could be split into three, each one of the three concentrating on a given word class.
Teaching intention	To enable pupils to revise the range of connectives which have been covered in the course of a term's work and to reinforce their knowledge within a context
Setting	Computer lab
Software required	Text-reconstruction software

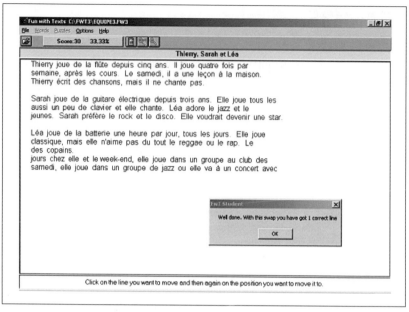

Getting at detail

Activity

- The teacher displays a text to the whole class. It consists of three short paragraphs, each paragraph containing three sentences. Some of the vocabulary is unfamiliar to the class, but discussion using context and knowledge of word clusters helps.
- Pupils are given five minutes to read quickly through the text to establish its gist and notes are made.
- They are then asked to read the first paragraph for detail.
- At the end of a further five minutes, they are invited to indicate words that they do not understand. Words which no one can understand are highlighted.
- This process is repeated with the remaining two paragraphs. Strategies are then adopted to work out the meaning of the unknown words, including the use of a dictionary.

- Pupils are invited to read each paragraph for detail again before the class votes on whether the gist was correctly detected.
- In a subsequent lesson pupils work on the same text, singly or in pairs, to re-order lines of the text and then to reconstruct it. Those for whom total reconstruction is difficult complete the text using multiple choice.

| *Teaching intention* | To pull together a number of different aspects of the work of a unit by involving pupils in gist reading and prediction, using context and word knowledge to get at detail and to bring into active use new knowledge acquired within a restricted context |

| *Setting* | Classroom with computer and projection facilities + computer lab |

| *Software required* | Word processor, *Text Salad* from *Fun with Texts* and text reconstruction (*Copywrite* from *Fun with Texts*) |

Combining a series of sentences to form a continuous text

| *Activity* | Pupils are given a continuous text composed of five complex sentences in which there are gaps for the connectives (e.g. and, but, when, if, because, when, where). They are required to fill the gaps. They then move on to a word-processed file which contains ten sentences in a logical order, which they are required to combine into a continuous text comprising of a maximum of five sentences. They then complete a similar task with new sentences, but this time the sentences are not in a logical order. |

| *Teaching intention* | To remind pupils of the role of five connectives and to give them practice in identifying their role within given sentences |

Setting	Computer lab

Software required	Gap-filling software and word processor

key points	• Pupils are used to working at the three levels of language – word, sentence and text. There is good availability of software to enable them to transfer their knowledge from the mother tongue to the target language
	• ICT offers a unique opportunity to move from reading to text reconstruction to writing in a highly motivating way
	• The key to improving pupil performance in the acquisition of knowledge, understanding and use of the target language is in the setting of appropriate tasks which challenge and engage
	• ICT media have their own characteristics which can promote learning. It is important to recognise those characteristics and exploit them appropriately

ICT for whole-class teaching in MFL

☐ What is 'whole-class teaching' in the current KS3 context?

☐ How can I use ICT for effective whole-class work in MFL?

☐ How can I exploit ICT to encourage pupils to develop their presentation skills?

chapter 4

What is 'whole-class teaching' in the current KS3 context?

The term 'whole-class teaching' no longer carries the traditional implication of the teacher standing at the front of the classroom and delivering the lesson objectives in a didactic manner – perhaps with the inclusion of a few questions to check whether pupils have remembered what they have been taught. What is meant currently by 'whole-class' or 'direct' teaching under the KS3 Strategies is significantly different. It suggests that teaching should be lively and promote the active involvement of pupils, it should provide challenge, extend thinking beyond simple questioning and exploit pupil responses for further learning. Questions which only have one response test simple memory skills, they do not offer opportunities for pupils to make links between different items of data. Furthermore, unless targeted at specific pupils (which can encourage other pupils to switch off!), such questioning techniques do not take an inclusive approach in a mixed-ability setting. Compare the following MFL examples, where the teacher is seeking a simple noun to introduce into a new structure:

Teacher: *Comment dit-on 'an apple' en français?* Pupil A: *Une pomme.*	Teacher: *Donnez-moi un fruit en français.* Pupil A: *Une orange.* Pupil B: *Une banane.* Pupil C: *Une pomme.* Pupil D: *Une fraise.* Pupil E: *Une pêche.* Teacher: *Très bien. Disons que j'ai une pomme …*

This is a simple example, but the advantages are clear. There is no wrong answer, so **all** pupils are encouraged to contribute what they can, with the obvious bonus of increased pupil engagement and, perhaps surprisingly, pace to the lesson. In seeking to respond, pupils are not trying to make the single link apple–*pomme* in their heads, but *fruit–pomme–banane–orange–fraise–pêche* and are likely to be silently translating the words, too.

The BECTA Web pages on pedagogy offer a definition of effective whole-class teaching:

High-quality direct teaching is oral, interactive and lively. It is not achieved by adopting a simplistic formula of 'drill and practice' and lecturing the class, or by expecting pupils to teach themselves from books. It is a two-way process in which pupils are expected to play an active part by answering questions, contributing points to discussions, and explaining and demonstrating their methods to the class.

The two-way process described enables pupils to accelerate their assimilation of information and consolidate their understanding through listening to their peers and experiencing their learning techniques.

Why use ICT?

How then can ICT support teachers and pupils to participate effectively in whole-class teaching? As discussed in Chapter 1, the range of media available can stimulate and provide support to a wide range of learning styles simultaneously. Visuals, both text and graphics, are clear to all and engaging. Pace can be maintained as the teacher is not required to waste time writing on the board or juggling countless flashcards, overhead transparencies and other props. The focus can be taken away from the teacher, encouraging participation from a wider range of pupils. By its very nature, presentation software such as PowerPoint lends itself to whole-class teaching and as such will feature frequently in this chapter. Most other types of software mentioned in this book will also have their place and it is obviously desirable to exploit a range of delivery media over time. This chapter will identify opportunities where ICT can add value to the delivery of lesson content (which is not necessarily at all points in the lesson!) and also to provide opportunities for pupils to take on the role of presenter.

The principles underpinning the KS3 Foundation Subjects Strategy listed on p3 provide a useful context within which to consider where ICT can enhance the delivery of MFL in a whole-class situation. On pp62–79 you will find a range of practical lesson ideas which exploit ICT listed under these headings. Before moving on to examine these activities, however, you may need to set up the required technology in a normal teaching classroom, if it is not available to you already. There is detailed information available on these technical options on the Web pages supporting this book (**www.cilt.org.uk/publications/impactonlearning**), where you simply need to click on one of the numerous links to be taken to manufacturers' websites in the field of projection and interactive whiteboard technology.

How can I use ICT for effective whole-class work in MFL?

As mentioned earlier, the **principles** and associated **actions** used in this chapter form the basis of the Foundation Subjects Strand and are consistent across the entire KS3 Strategy. Whether or not you embark upon KS3 Strategy training for MFL at your school, these principles offer a useful checklist for any MFL teacher and set a context within which to examine each of the following applications of ICT to effective MFL teaching and learning. The activities described assume access either to an interactive whiteboard or to a computer, data projector and large screen.

Principle	*Focus the teaching*
Action	*Plan according to objectives and ensure pupils know what they are*

Explicit learning objectives

A significant factor in successful teaching is the need to be explicit about the learning objectives for a particular lesson. Learning should not be about coverage, but about mastery and where MFL is concerned, this does not refer simply to the mastery of vocabulary and structures. Learning how to learn languages will prove equally valuable in the long term, as future linguistic needs cannot be predicted. The National Curriculum Programme of Study still provides an excellent reference point for the articulation of these skills. Advances in literacy teaching in KS1 and KS2 have aimed at developing more linguistically aware pupils, which MFL teachers should build on in KS3 with an explicit approach to objectives. The Developing Cultural Awareness area of the Programme of Study should also be reflected wherever possible.

The use of more explicit language to talk about language raises the question of whether learning objectives should be presented in English or in the TL. The sensible approach would seem to be that where explanations can be made in accessible TL, it should be used. ICT can provide a means of increasing this accessibility, simply by providing written support to the teacher's introduction of the objectives, in summary form and with key words highlighted. If PowerPoint or other presentation software is used, each objective can be brought on screen at the relevant point, guiding pupils through the monologue. Translations of new key words can also be displayed, without the teacher having to revert to speaking in English.

Vous allez:
- *apprendre de nouveaux mots sur le thème de la nourriture;*   *[sur le thème de = on the topic of]*

- *lire et comprendre le sens de nouveaux mots par le contexte;*
- *découvrir le petit déjeuner typique des Français;*   *[découvrir = find about about]*

- *décrire votre petit déjeuner à votre partenaire.*

Clear instructions

The KS3 Strategy also highlights the need for clarity in directions given by the teacher. The opportunity to display typewritten text, rather than teacher handwriting (which can vary in clarity!), is an obvious advantage – particularly as it comes in a range of font sizes and line widths. Some of the interactive whiteboard (IW) technologies also provide a handwriting recognition facility within their software, so when the teacher writes normally on the board with the IW 'pen', it is automatically converted to type. Note that this will not work perfectly for all languages, particularly those in non-Roman script.

A further advantage is that the teacher need not rely on talking through instructions for completing a worksheet, assuming that it has been word processed. The worksheet can be displayed on screen and sample answers completed in front of all pupils, which is likely to be recalled with more success than via oral instructions. Teacher talk can focus more on the linguistic strategies pupils should be considering when completing answers, rather than on the activity instructions themselves. This is true of any electronic exercise. Where access to a suite of computers is limited and time is therefore at a premium, teachers could consider preparing pupils in the preceding classroom-based lesson, by going through the electronic activities on screen.

Principle ▸ *Make explicit concepts and conventions*

Action ▸ *Use questioning, explaining, modelling*

Manipulating word order

The flexibility of electronic text can be exploited, for example, to help pupils internalise the changes caused in a sentence by the introduction of *weil* to link two sentences in German. On paper we can simply highlight the ultimate changes:

> *Ich habe Katzen gern. Sie sind freundlich.*
> *Ich habe Katzen gern,* **weil** *sie freundlich* **sind***.*

However, most pupils will be assisted in internalising the concept much more quickly if these changes can be represented more visually and physically, particularly those pupils with a leaning towards a visual and/or kinaesthetic learning style. The ability to drag and drop words around in the 'lesson' software which comes with an interactive whiteboard is an obvious opportunity. Pupils can watch as the teacher talks through the following in TL:

- the full stop is deleted; the capital letter of *Sie* is replaced with a small *s;*
- a comma is added after *gern* (as needed before *weil*);
- *weil* is added after the comma;
- the verb is highlighted, dragged out of its place and dropped back in at the end of the sentence.

Words affected by the change to the sentence can be highlighted in colour. Pupils can then come to the front and try examples themselves, possibly with peer guidance from the floor! This is most effective on an interactive whiteboard using the integral software, but if you don't have an interactive whiteboard, pupils can just come up and use the mouse (or use an optical remote mouse from their seat). This type of word manipulation can also be done effectively in Normal view in PowerPoint or in Word using text boxes – remember that you can go to Format > Text Box > Fill to give your text boxes background colour for greater visibility. Using a different Fill colour for the words you wish to focus on would also help to reinforce the changes made to word order.

| Ich | habe | Katzen | gern | , | weil | sie | freundlich | sind | . |

Presenting grammar step by step

A PowerPoint presentation lends itself well to step-by-step explanation of grammar as slides are fixed in a linear pattern and information can be built up in stages. There is also the advantage that visual tools such as colour and images can be used to set the context, reinforce concepts and support TL use. For example, when introducing partitive articles in French, the concept of gender has to be reinforced before the new language is taught.

- Noun vocabulary can be revised initially, pictures on screen prompting oral suggestions from pupils and actively engaging them. When the written form appears on screen as feedback, it can be coloured according to its gender (e.g red = feminine and blue = masculine).
- The structure *je voudrais* can be introduced and discussed to establish the need for a partitive element to follow – images subsequently used could also emphasise the concept of 'part of a whole' where appropriate.
- The feminine concept could be dealt with first – a *de* coloured in red could appear to complete the gap between *Je voudrais* and *la pizza* (also cloured red).
- A similar slide could be used for *le gâteau* but when *de* appears, alarm bells are heard. Pupils see the *de* and *le* crawl off screen and *du* coloured in blue appear in its place. (In earlier versions of PowerPoint, you can create the effect of items moving by copying and pasting an item repeatedly, each pasted a short distance from the last.)
- A similar slide with colour coding used for both *les bonbons* (m) and *les fraises* (f) on the same slide would follow.

As you need to invest time in sourcing images and reinforcing concepts in this way, it makes sense to incorporate follow-up practice exercises into the presentation, with the inclusion of several question slides at the end using the same images and symbols. The provision of optional Action Buttons with hyperlinks linking back to the 'alarm bell' slides could be useful when going through these answers in a whole-class situation, should revision be required (go to Slide Show > Action Buttons).

Vocabulary introduction

PowerPoint is also useful for creating 'virtual flashcards'. They have the disadvantage that pupils cannot handle them and pass them around the classroom, but once created, you can print them out in colour and laminate them. Effectively, you can use the software as a design package, allowing for both on-screen and off-screen use.

In a 'virtual flashcards' context, pupils can see the picture and are given the opportunity to associate sound with meaning. Immediately afterwards you can present the written word as an overlay, which is much more cumbersome when working with normal flashcards. Furthermore, when introducing vocabulary for verbs, you can use animation clips to emphasise that the word represents an action. The linear structure of a PowerPoint presentation means that you can devise memory games of the 'what word came next' type – this can take away the advantage from your linguistically most-gifted for once and enable others to provide the answers! You can also revise vocabulary by showing small sections of the original visual image, again introducing an element of memory testing beyond the TL vocabulary and assisting pupils in associating the image with the word.

Analysing written text

The facility of ICT for displaying legible text in a whole-class situation allows for shared textual analysis and a step-by-step visual record of the exercise, which should support the development of sophisticated analytical skills earlier than they might usually be tackled. This type of exercise is not as viable when pupils are focused downwards on separate paper copies where they cannot make deletions, change the font size, move text around nor use different colours easily, for example.

Appropriate text received in the form of an e-mail from a partner school or from an official agency would constitute a welcome authentic approach to this activity. Interactive whiteboard software would allow you to annotate directly onto the text, of course, but some e-mail programmes also offer considerable flexibility.

Principle	*Support pupils' application and independent learning*
Action	*Use prompts, frames and other forms of support and targeted intervention*

Information on the TL country

MFL teachers are now being encouraged to present more concrete information about the TL country than they might have done previously, which introduces the need for use of more specialised vocabulary. Presentation software can be effectively exploited to support pupils' listening comprehension skills and strategies for coping with unknown language in this context. The two slides on p68 are taken from a German presentation on the Berlin Wall to an upper set of Year 9 pupils.

Illustrations reduce the need for English translation and set a more memorable context, often providing useful cultural background at the same time. Keywords can be highlighted or translated on screen and can be introduced one by one by clicking the mouse at appropriate points and the timed introduction of points can guide pupils through the oral presentation. The slide examples shown on p68 could be differentiated by reducing the amount of text on each slide. Simply create the first slide with two or three keywords then go to Insert > Duplicate Slide, edit accordingly and repeat as necessary.

Don't forget the option of inserting digital video files into a PowerPoint presentation should you have built up such resources through trips abroad or if you have located useful clips on the Internet (go to Insert > Movies and Sounds > Movie from file). It is worth noting that some (often smaller) publishers are also starting to offer resource banks of digital video clips for sale. The potential for introducing more regular exposure to the TL culture in this way is significant as brief clips can be played on the click of a mouse. Formerly, this may have involved wheeling a TV and video down a corridor, plugging in a series of wires and winding through a video tape to find the relevant segment, which tended to result in the sole use of longer recordings used on an infrequent basis. Techniques for exploiting video in both a whole-class and independent learning situation are explored in detail in the CILT publication InfoTech 4: *Video in language learning* (Hill 1999).

Slides from a Year 9 PowerPoint presentation

Develop well-paced lessons with high levels of interaction

Use collaborative tasks and talk for learning

Flexible records of discussion

The elements of questioning and discussing have been touched upon many times already as they should infiltrate everything we do in the classroom. It is worth focusing briefly on discrete brainstorming sessions, however, as we exploit these frequently in MFL lessons to concentrate pupils on a topic, to get them thinking and talking in the TL and to help them organise their thoughts. Almost invariably we make a written record on the whiteboard or flipchart as the discussion develops, circling items and drawing arrows to identify priorities and/or categories and to make connections between ideas. While this may have been more the domain of KS4 GCSE topic work in the past, teachers are being encouraged more and more to develop pupils' thinking skills, to which such an activity supported with visual mapping lends itself well. Very often, however, this valuable record of shared thought processes is lost to the board eraser or waste bin or becomes an illegible scrawl.

Here, the facility for annotation within interactive whiteboard software can be invaluable as it offers the facility to save and/or print out such a 'document', for pupils to access at their leisure. There are also a number of useful flow charts and diagrams available in Word XP/2002, which can be exploited for brainstorming or representing concepts (go to Insert > Diagram). If you are working with an earlier version of Microsoft Office, you can insert an Organisation Chart into a PowerPoint slide (Insert > Picture > Organisation Chart) and then copy and paste the chart graphic into Word. By clicking on it you will open up MS Organisation Chart software, which you can maximise to full screen. You can then edit the text and add branches as desired. The length of each text entry is limited by cell size restrictions, but the benefits to pupils of being able to return to the physical outcomes of a discussion and to edit it according to their needs are significant. If funds are available, it might also be worth investigating commercial 'mind mapping' software such as *Inspiration* from Research Machines to facilitate whole-class oral work.

Sorting ideas

Another approach to try is the use of Outline View in Word (go to View > Outline before you start typing). This will not allow complex linking between ideas, but it will offer pupils the opportunity to brainstorm ideas and then sort elements into categories and then to prioritise them within categories – without lots of copying and pasting. Elements appear in bullet point form and the Demote function relegates items to sub-topic status, whereas Promote can be used to establish headings. You can then Move Up and Down elements to re-order them as the pupils watch. Font colour can be used, of course, to track items as they are moved up and down.

- For example, you might have brainstormed a list of food items which the class generally likes and then a list of those which are unpopular with the class, colouring those food items which are less popular in a different colour.
- You might then wish to sort items into 'healthy' and 'unhealthy' categories.
- Following on, you could prioritise items within categories according to how good or bad they are for you. Each time you are expecting pupils to engage with the nature of the vocabulary, not just process it 'parrot-fashion', which should assist the internalisation process.
- This also offers many opportunities for the painless introduction and manipulation of comparative structures in context. You will end up with a clear visual overview of whether pupils' likes and dislikes correspond to a healthy eating lifestyle!

You can save the final document on the network for pupils to access for revision or editing for their own needs, such as into a vocabulary list with English translations or a personalised list of likes and dislikes.

Voting systems

The existence of sophisticated 'voting technology' as an optional peripheral to some interactive whiteboard products must be mentioned in the context of effective questioning. Pupils are given handsets with voting buttons, which can be programmed in various ways – for example, they can be set in 'anonymous' mode or each handset can be identified with a particular pupil. After introducing a point of new language, the teacher can ask a closed question with a series of multiple-choice answers. Pupils are then given twenty seconds to register their answer by clicking either A, B, C or D, for example, in a system not dissimilar from that used on the popular TV show 'Who wants to be a millionaire?'. The teacher gets immediate feedback as to what percentage of the class has opted for each answer – this has obvious advantages for formative assessment over asking for a show of hands as to who has understood. When data is linked to individual pupils, the teacher can collate and print out the data on each pupil at the end of a lesson, which can be a valuable contribution to the assessment process.

Principle	*Make learning active*
Action	*Provide tasks in which pupils make meaning, construct knowledge and develop understanding and skills through problem solving, investigation and enquiry*

Developing data-processing skills

Towards the end of KS3, pupils will extend their ICT work in data-processing to the design and construction of simple datafiles. A datafile consists of a series of fields which need to be completed, which very often equates to a series of questions which need an answer. In MFL lessons TL surveys are often conducted but they do not always result in concrete outcomes. If the outcome of a survey is to be the construction of a class datafile, however, there is great potential for whole-class discussion on the kind of information pupils might want to collect on a particular topic, which would then need to be formulated into questions and a basic datafile structure. This can involve significant logistical problem solving, if you are new to the discipline! This cognitive engagement and ownership of the project from the start will create a new dimension to survey work for many teachers and their pupils. Once data has been collected and entered into the datafile, fields can be browsed and predictions made as a whole class. These predictions can then be investigated by subsequent interrogation of the datafile. The research base could also be extended beyond the classroom, by sending a questionnaire to a partner class in the TL country, for example. See Chapter 2 for a more detailed example of a data-processing activity.

Principle	Structure the learning
Action	**Use starters and plenaries and a clear lesson structure**

Slow-reveal pictures

A very simple activity you can set up to stimulate spontaneous discussion is to reveal segments of a picture one by one. Pupils can be encouraged to describe orally in the TL what they see and then to speculate as to what the picture may show as a whole. If the picture and stages of exposure are chosen carefully, this speculation will change each time. This is an ideal opportunity to introduce images from the TL country, particularly those which will lead to a comparison between the UK way of life and that of the TL country. It could also be a useful starter activity to lead pupils into a new topic or to revise adjectives of colour, for example.

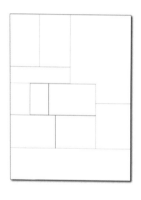

The easiest way to reveal a picture in this way is to use a series of PowerPoint slides. Insert the picture on the first slide and then cover it with a number of AutoShape Rectangles, with the rectangle border lines removed (Format > AutoShape > No line). Then go to Insert Duplicate Slide and delete one rectangle from an appropriate place to reveal a small part of the picture. This action then needs to be repeated on subsequent duplicate slides until all rectangles have been removed. When you present the activity to pupils, they simply see a part of the picture revealed each time you click. There is also an effective 'Spotlight' facility available in some interactive whiteboard software, which allows for an alternative approach to the same activity – the screen is blacked out except for a small hole, which can be moved around by dragging the 'pen' to reveal different parts of the picture. Likewise, a 'blind' can be placed over the screen and pulled down to expose a page line by line, as you would reveal an OHT in stages.

'Open' vocabulary revision

This exercise can be completed in Excel, Access or other types of data-processing package, but is perhaps easiest to set up in Word. Simply insert a table with columns for gender marker, TL word, English word and word type, as required. Instead of giving pupils a vocabulary test at the end of a unit, which involves closed questions to test simple memory skills, try asking the class to remember as many words as they can from the topic. As words are suggested, you can ask pupils to spell it out loud, translate it, tell you the gender where relevant, tell you what type of word it is (e.g. *nom, adjectif, verbe*) etc. You would decide what is completed in full at this stage to balance the needs of accuracy, focus and pace – it can always be edited and expanded after the lesson.

If you create a table in this way, the data can then be manipulated by sorting columns into alphabetical order. This means pupils can sort words into gender groups, make a list of adjectives, create an English to TL glossary and vice versa, etc. Pupils can also customise their copy, by highlighting all the words they cannot write out from memory, for example, which makes it an extremely flexible resource.

Genre	Français	Anglais	Mot
	noir(e)	black	adjectif
	bleu(e)	blue	adjectif
	brun(e)	brown	adjectif
	vert(e)	green	adjectif
	long(ue)	long	adjectif
	rouge	red	adjectif
	court(e)	short	adjectif
	blanc(he)	white	adjectif
	jaune	yellow	adjectif
le	chemisier	blouse	nom
la	chemise	shirt	nom
la	jupe	skirt	nom
les (f)	chaussettes	socks	nom
le	pantalon	trousers	nom
les (f)	chaussures	shoes	verbe
	détester	to hate	verbe
	aimer	to like	verbe
	s'habiller	to put on (clothes)	verbe
	porter	to wear	verbe

Note that sorting of the TL column will work only with Roman script languages. Compromise solutions for non-Roman scripts might be to use a romanised version of the language or to write the transliteration of the first part of the word before the TL script (e.g. *shuu* しゅうまつ for 'weekend' in Japanese), although these solutions will only respect the order of the English alphabet. The facility to sort the other columns will still be of significant benefit, however.

CD-ROM and other interactive software

Surprisingly, a valuable resource for exploitation in a whole-class situation is the multimedia CD-ROM, a medium usually associated with independent learning because of its facility for individual feedback. Pupils can come to the front to try out their answer or give instructions to a pupil acting as 'teacher'. The focus is taken from the teacher onto the 'neutral' computer, and as judgments on pupil answers seem to be less personal, pupils are often encouraged to participate more actively and to take more risks. The teacher can intervene to ask a pupil how he or she arrived at the correct answer. The question can then be extended to other pupils who reached the same correct conclusion but via a different stream of thought, encouraging pupils to reflect on their learning and reinforce understanding. Techniques for exploiting multimedia are explored in depth in the CILT publication InfoTech 6: *Multimedia in language learning* (Slater and Varney-Burch 2001).

When choosing software, you must decide whether you want software which links in very closely with your textbook, or whether you want to explore new contexts and vary the pupil diet. Your Scheme of Work, differentiation needs and teaching style must also be considered. The size of text font must also be taken into account if you wish to use it in a whole class situation. Good evaluation skills are therefore crucial and have been a focus of the New Opportunities Fund (NOF) and subsequent training initiatives. This has resulted in provision both of rich guidance in this area and of software reviews, such as TEEM (Teachers Evaluating Educational Media), ICT4LT (ICT for Language Teachers) and the BECTA Educational Software Database. CILT also provides an on-line database listing of MFL software held in its library and although aimed mainly at KS2, NACELL's database also includes software, much of which will be valuable for Year 7 work. The DfES Curriculum Online website provides listings of software categorised according to the National Curriculum Programme of Study.

Such listings will also include titles of authoring software, such as those described in Chapter 3 – this is an area where departmental collaboration is crucial! As well as those you author yourself, ready-made interactive exercises can be sourced on the Web and exploited in a whole-class context, if a live Internet connection is available. Try looking, for example, at *The Guardian* **Learn.co.uk** site, which has extensive ready-made activities in French, and also at UK school websites with an MFL resources section. You will also find useful MFL sites listed on the DfES Virtual Teacher Centre website.

Principle ▶ *Build reflection*

Action ▶ *Teach pupils to think about what and how they learn, and involve them in setting targets for future lessons*

Pupils using PowerPoint for consolidating learning

Pupils can exploit PowerPoint to structure their own reflections on learning. The step-by-step creation of slides and the inherent decisions required force pupils to consider and resolve a range of problems:

- what order should information be presented in;
- how can knowledge be divided into manageable chunks;
- what are the links between one point and the next;
- which examples should be given;
- how can we make them accurate and clear enough for a critical audience.

As we know ourselves, as teachers, the process of preparing and teaching something to a second party can reveal unexpected new insights. This type of activity will be even more valuable when pupils are encouraged to work in pairs or groups, as the negotiation process will deepen their thinking. The delivery of such a presentation in front of the class holds significant benefits for the development of pupil skills, which is considered further on p79.

It is also useful to refer back to Learning Objectives at the end of a lesson in the context of assessing outcomes – this will lend value to the setting of them, while also highlighting progress made. This can be done very effectively by revisiting the simple presentation mentioned on p63 and taking the time to reflect in an explicit way on **how** each objective has been met and the different strategies available for retaining the knowledge, which may well be done in English. Lesson outcomes should also be linked to the learning which will take place in the next lesson, both in terms of language-learning skills and linguistic content.

The World Wide Web for pupil choice

As well as offering up-to-date and authentic material not available in textbooks, the Web offers a range and scope of material beyond the reach of the school library or departmental photocopying budget. This feature can be exploited for offering pupils choice in learning resources. This can help to develop a positive attitude to language learning as pupils are given the opportunity to explore and can enjoy ownership of and engagement with their work, a sense of independence and responsibility and are encouraged to read for pleasure in line with their own interests. When asked to present their findings in a whole-class situation, the information and experience they offer constitute a genuine sharing of knowledge and should therefore be of interest to others!

There are some rich TL websites aimed at young people in the TL country, for example the French **Momes.net** site, which contains letters, poems, reports, film reviews and discussions on a huge range of topics at the KS2/KS3 level – many contributed by children. A look at the *Comptines* section under *Animaux* reveals eight poems based solely on rabbits; the example on the right was contributed by 'Sandrine'.

Mon petit lapin

J'ai un petit lapin
Qui mange du pain
J'ai un petit lapin
Qui mange du thym

Mais un lapin ça fait des crottes,
Un jour, il a fait dans mes bottes.

Maman dit que c'est un vilain,
Moi je dis que c'est mon copain.

MOMES.NET

The process pupils will undertake to select such a poem involves reading for gist, evaluating texts for language level and deciding on their suitability for the prospective audience, which involves deeper engagement than with a traditional paper-based reading comprehension. The next stage sees pupils examining detail, coping with unknown language, investigating pronunciation with the teacher or FLA, using dictionary strategies and trying out different approaches to translation, as you would expect.

The authentic nature of the text means that a wide range of linguistic awareness can be developed. In the French example above, pupils discover that different letter groups can have the same sound, that colloquial language is often used to refer to toilet habits as we do in English, that simple literary techniques can increase the impact of writing and that mothers and their children see things differently in the TL culture, as is so in our own.

As pupils work to prepare their presentation, teachers can intervene and offer constructive advice as they circulate the classroom. You are more likely to spot linguistic errors in work on screen than you might when pupils are working on paper. The presentation by a pupil or group of pupils can involve a combination of the elements below:

- a practised reading aloud of the poem in the TL;
- a polished translation in English;
- an explanation of difficult and/or interesting TL terms;
- a justification for choosing the poem;
- a continuation of the poem by the pupil;
- an adaptation of the poem to feature another animal and rhyming pattern;
- an imaginary short speech by the person who wrote the poem.

Such elements provide for stimulating whole-class discussion, as pupils will be interested in what their peers have chosen and the content of their presentation. It is not ideal to try to feature every pupil's presentation on every occasion, but it is vital to keep an ongoing record, to make sure all pupils get their turn over time. A certificate or observation slip (on carbon copy) with brief written comments on the positive aspects of a presentation and selected pointers for future improvement would be a useful record for pupils. This could go into their Record of Achievement and teachers would keep their own copy. Another approach is to video each presentation if facilities are available and get pupils to watch themselves for the purpose of self-assessment. Either way, teachers should aim only to point out recurring or particularly bad mistakes to the individual pupil(s) and to make a note of more widespread errors to feed explicitly into future teaching.

How can I exploit ICT to encourage pupils to develop their presentation skills?

Self-confidence is a quality which seems to characterise largely successful language learners, whereas a lack of self-confidence will lower the level of pupil performance. By experiencing failure, pupil reluctance to speak grows, both when in front of the class and in plenary sessions. They may well, however, find oral presentation easier and more rewarding if they are taught to exploit presentation software such as PowerPoint to develop their skills and confidence.

As described on p76, the thinking processes pupils must go through to produce a set of PowerPoint slides help to internalise the logical content of a speech. Pupil oral presentations (and likewise GCSE oral work) often originate as a written piece which does not always lend itself well to oral performance. Preparing a speech as a series of slides rather than as a block of prose will help to avoid this phenomenon and result in a performance more appropriate for an audience, as pupils consider the potential listeners as they prepare. Those who struggle to produce clear handwriting will experience particular benefit from the use of ICT in this context.

Talking to a PowerPoint presentation provides a pre-prepared structure for the thoughts the speaker wishes to convey. As writing frames help provide pupils with content guidelines, so slides help to provide the content for speaking. Pupils can be very daunted when presenting to their peers and minds sometimes go blank, resulting in failure. The visual content of a PowerPoint presentation can therefore also be very valuable, particularly for those who prefer a visual learning style. The use of pictures to prompt content can also support pupils who are good auditory learners and prefer to link the sounds of words to meaning rather than the written form. Pupils also avoid the extra time needed to read and internalise text, which can be particularly important for those less comfortable working with the written word. Inclusion also of bullet-point text can provide the key TL vocabulary for each slide, should extra reinforcement be needed.

Not only will such support improve performance, it will also assist the pupil audience watching and listening. Pupil pronunciation may not always be as accessible as that of a TL model and where language has been personalised, vocabulary new to the audience may be used. This new vocabulary and key words can be translated on screen where necessary. The more engaged the audience appears, the more responsive and naturally animated the presenter is likely to be. The pupil will not be looking down at rough notes on a scruffy piece of paper in his or her hand, but looking up towards the audience and/or pointing at the projected screen, if direct eye contact is too threatening. Where pupils have worked in pairs, one can speak while the other clicks the mouse or interactive whiteboard 'pen' at appropriate points, which means both are engaged in the presentation. It can be worthwhile involving the pupil audience further by means of peer assessment based on a printed list of criteria, such as ease of understanding, the amount of recycled language used, the visual impact of the presentation, etc. Such peer assessment will not only engage pupils more in reflection on what has been learned, but will also reinforce the message that language learning develops the valuable skills of effective communication.

Once pupils have started to develop their presentation skills, any other less-structured software tool can be exploited, as their use still enjoys most of the benefits mentioned above. For example, an oral presentation could consist of a description of a pie chart displayed to the class in Word, or an explanation of the route taken through a website. Setting up a classroom for the use of ICT in a whole-class context can therefore result in a much richer teaching and learning experience for teachers and pupils alike.

key points	• Whole-class teaching is most effective when pupils interact with the teacher and with one another
	• The extra support from ICT facilities for the whole ability range enables the teacher to progress more quickly in a whole-class setting and to set more challenging tasks
	• Investigate the range of options for enabling the use of ICT with the whole class, as at least one or two should be realistic for most schools
	• ICT offers significant opportunities for supporting the development of pupil skills and self-confidence in presentation
	• A wide range of ICT applications can be exploited to promote different elements of the Foundation Subjects Strand of the KS3 Strategy

Conclusion

This book has focused on three key areas which have a significant contribution to make to raising standards in MFL in KS3 – the development of study skills, word-processing and text manipulation and whole class teaching and learning. The specific features of ICT highlighted throughout this book, such as the simultaneous appeal of an activity to a range of learning styles or the facility lent to teachers to differentiate and support pupils more fully within a lesson, are already having a marked impact on pupil attainment (DfES/BECTA 2002). Indications for MFL are very positive and research is continuing in this field. Pupils have an entitlement to benefit from the added value ICT can bring and this book has sought to identify when and how the application of ICT is appropriate and useful in MFL teaching and learning.

With more linguistically aware pupils entering Year 7, reflection on the characteristics of effective language learners is even more worthwhile and ICT offers ways of enhancing or facilitating the development of such characteristics in all pupils. Where pupils are challenged, are taught to apply learning strategies consciously and are encouraged to engage in deeper cognitive processes, they are more likely to internalise language and skills ready for future manipulation. With thoughtful exploitation of relatively low-tech programs such as word processing, we can have significant impact on pupils' work at Word, Sentence and Text level, underpinning the principles of the KS3 Strategy at all times. Again, the extension of activity types, differentiation opportunities and facilities for more targeted feedback offered by ICT can move pupils on much more quickly through their learning at KS3 and through their MFL scheme(s) of work.

It is not to say that the three focus areas of this book are the only contexts where ICT has a role to play. The volume of generic software, MFL-specific software, hardware and non-computer based ICT is vast. The extensive potential of ICT for communication, for example, has only been touched upon, yet what it has to offer in terms of developing skills of social interaction and the creative application of language is significant. The range of examples given of ICT in whole-class teaching offer a flavour of this potential and all focus on maximising interaction within the classroom, which is reflected by the current interest in interactive whiteboard technology. As this technology can enhance the use of any form of software you can run on a computer and which works well in a whole-class teaching context, its potential is far reaching and likely to feature in discussion of MFL-ICT pedagogy in years to come. The very breadth of ICT available, software and hardware alike, makes it all the more crucial that MFL colleagues work as a department and within clusters of schools on the development and maintenance of teaching resources and in their continuing professional development.

As DfES policy moves more towards supporting the use of ICT in subject teaching (DfES 2003) and continues to invest in ICT in schools, along with the advent of more explicit guidance at KS3 in the form of the Framework for MFL, teachers of MFL should have more and more opportunities to extend their practice in this field and this key stage. It is our hope that this book has provided a useful context to build from and a wide enough range of practical ideas to inspire you to create further opportunities to raise the achievement of your KS3 pupils in MFL.

List of websites

British Educational Communications and Technology Agency (BECTA):
www.becta.org.uk
BECTA Educational Software Database (BESD): http://besd.becta.org.uk
Health and safety: www.ictadvice.org.uk/index.php?rid=151
ImpaCT2 research report: www.becta.org.uk/research/reports/impact2/index.cfm
Presentation technologies: www.becta.org.uk/teaching/pedagogy/technologies
Say IT information sheets: www.becta.org.uk/technology/sayit/index.html
SEN specialist software: www.becta.org.uk/inclusion
Whole class pedagogy: www.becta.org.uk/teaching/pedagogy

Camsoft: www.camsoftpartners.co.uk
Fun with Texts: www.camsoftpartners.co.uk/fwt.htm
Gapkit: www.camsoftpartners.co.uk/gapkit.htm

CILT, the National Centre for Languages: www.cilt.org.uk
Continuing Professional Development (ICT): www.cilt.org.uk/cpd/ict.htm
Library catalogue: www.cilt.org.uk/libcat/index.htm
Publications (ICT): www.cilt.org.uk/publications/ICT.htm
New Pathfinder 3 companion website: www.cilt.org.uk/publications/impactonlearning

Crick software: www.cricksoft.com/uk
Clicker: www.cricksoft.com/uk/clicker_products/index.htm

Curriculum Online: www.curriculumonline.gov.uk

Granada Learning: www.granada-learning.com
En Route/Unterwegs: www.granada-learning.com/school (see Catalogue Secondary > MFL)

Guardian **Learn.co.uk: www.learn.co.uk**

Heinemann: www.heinemann.co.uk
Métro Electro: www.heinemann.co.uk/secondary (see Modern Languages > French)

Hot Potatoes: http://web.uvic.ca/hrd/halfbaked

ICT for Language Teachers (ICT4LT): www.ict4lt.org
Evaluating CALL software: www.ict4lt.org/en/en_mod1-4.htm#eval
Writing for the screen: www.ict4lt.org/en/en_mod3-2.htm#writing

ICT in Schools, DfES: www.dfes.gov.uk/ictinschools
Fulfilling the Potential: www.dfes.gov.uk/ictinschools/docs/fulfilling_potential.pdf

Kindernetz: **www.kindernetz.de**
Forum: www.kindernetz.de/wohnpark/foren

Languages Strategy, DfES: www.dfes.gov.uk/languagesstrategy

Learn.co.uk, **The Guardian: www.learn.co.uk**

Lingu@NET forum: www.mailbase.org.uk/lists/linguanet-forum

Mômes: www.momes.net
Comptines: www.momes.net/comptines/index.html

National Advisory Centre on Early Language Learning: www.nacell.org.uk
Teaching Materials database: www.nacell.org.uk/resources/search/search.jsp

National Curriculum Online: www.nc.uk.net

National Grid for Learning: www.ngfl.gov.uk

New Opportunities Fund (NOF): www.nof.org.uk (see Education > ICT Training for
Teachers ...)

RM: www.rm.com
Inspiration: www.rm.com/Secondary/Products/Product.asp?cref=PD552

Standards site, DfES: www.standards.dfes.gov.uk
KS3 Framework for Teaching MFL: www.standards.dfes.gov.uk/keystage3/publications
KS3 National Strategy: www.standards.dfes.gov.uk/keystage3
KS3 Schemes of Work (MFL and ICT): www.standards.dfes.gov.uk/schemes
Learning Styles and Writing (in MFL): www.standards.dfes.gov.uk/keystage3/publications
National Literacy Strategy: www.standards.dfes.gov.uk/literacy
National Numeracy Strategy: www.standards.dfes.gov.uk/numeracy

Superhighway Safety, DfES: http://safety.ngfl.gov.uk
Intellectual property and copyright: http://safety.ngfl.gov.uk/schools/
document.php3?D=d10

TeacherNet: www.teachernet.gov.uk

Teacher Resource Exchange: http://tre.ngfl.gov.uk

Teachers Evaluating Educational Multimedia (TEEM): www.teem.org.uk

Virtual Teacher Centre: www.vtc.ngfl.gov.uk
MFL subject resources: http://vtc.ngfl.gov.uk/docserver.php?temid=160

WIDA Software: www.wida.co.uk
The Authoring Suite: www.wida.co.uk/auth

Widgit Software: www.widgit.com
Writing with Symbols 2000: www.widgit.com/html/products/modern-foreign-
language.html

Wordlearn: www.brainsystems.com

References

Bloom, B. S. (1956) *Taxonomy of educational objectives: the classification of educational goals.* Longmans, Green.

Buckland, D. (2000) InfoTech 5: *Putting achievement first.* CILT.

DfES (2002) *Key Stage 3 National Strategy: Learning styles and writing in Modern Foreign Languages.* DfES Publications.

DfES (2002) *Learning styles and writing in MFL.* DfES Publications.

DfES (2003) *Fulfilling the potential – transforming teaching and learning through ICT in schools.* DfES Publications.

DfES/BECTA (2002) *ImpaCT2 – the impact of information and communication technologies on pupil learning and attainment.* DfES Publications.

Gardner, H. (1983) *Frames of mind: the theory of multiple intelligences.* New York: Basic Books.

Gläsmann, S. (2004) InfoTech 7: *Communicating on-line.* CILT.

Hill, B. (1999) InfoTech 4: *Video in language learning.* CILT.

Rendall, H. (2003) *Harnessing the power of the computer – electronic worksheets.* IAT MFL WR6 6YG.

Rubin, J. (1975) 'What the good language learner can teach us.' *TESOL Quarterly,* Vol. 9, No. 1.

Rubin, J. (1981) 'Study of cognitive processes in second language learning'. *Applied Linguistics,* Vol. 11, No. 2.

Slater, P. and Varney-Burch, S. (2001) InfoTech 6: *Multimedia in language learning.* CILT.

Stern, H. (1975) 'What can we learn from the good language learner?' *Canadian Modern Languages Review:* 304-318.

classic pathfinder

timeless topics for all MFL teachers

Classic Pathfinders deal with those MFL issues that will never go away. Based on the wisdom contained in the best-selling titles in the *Pathfinder* series, the material has been re-written and updated by the original authors in the light of the challenges of today's classroom. Each title contains re-editions of two related titles in the *Pathfinder* range which are truly 'classic'.

Classic Pathfinders are for:

- experienced teachers refreshing or renewing their practice – particularly as they go into positions of leadership and need to articulate the principles of good practice;
- newly qualified or beginner teachers who want to build up the essentials of good language-teaching methodology.

Classic Pathfinder 1

You speak, they speak: focus on target language use

Barry Jones, Susan Halliwell and Bernardette Holmes

Classic Pathfinder 2

Challenging classes: focus on pupil behaviour

Jenifer Alison and Susan Halliwell

Classic Pathfinder 3

Inspiring performance: focus on drama and song

Judith Hamilton, Anne McLeod and Steven Fawkes

New Pathfinders

provide an expert MFL perspective on national initiatives. They are designed to support the language-teaching profession by ensuring that MFL has its own voice and ideas on the issues in education today.

New Pathfinders provide user-friendly support, advice and reference material for today's CPD agenda.

New Pathfinder 1

Raising the standard: addressing the needs of gifted and talented pupils

Anneli McLachlan

New Pathfinder 2

The language of success: improving grades at GCSE

Dave Carter

New Pathfinder 3

Impact on learning: what ICT can bring to MFL in KS3

Claire Dugard and Sue Hewer